Aesop's Fables

AESOP'S FABLES

AESOP

ILLUSTRATED BY
ERNEST GRISET

INTRODUCTION AND NOTES BY
EDWARD W. CLAYTON

BARNES & NOBLE
NEW YORK

SIGNATURE B&N EDITIONS

BARNES & NOBLE

NEW YORK

387 Park Avenue South
New York, NY 10016

ISBN 978-1-4351-3630-4 (print format)
ISBN 978-1-4351-4100-1 (ebook)

CONTENTS

List of Illustrations

The Life and Times of Aesop

Note that many of these dates are uncertain or represent best estimates and that some of the individuals included here may not have existed at all (Homer, Hesiod, and Aesop).

BCE

ca. 1400   The oracle at Delphi is founded.

ca. 1200   The Trojan War takes place.

ca. 1000   King David establishes Jerusalem as the capital of Israel.

776   The first Olympic Games are held.

753   The legendary founding of Rome takes place.

ca. 750   The Greek alphabet is created.

The *Iliad* and *Odyssey* are composed; attributed to Homer, they are the oldest surviving works of Greek literature.

ca. 700   Attributed to Hesiod, *Works and Days* and *Theogony* are composed.

ca. 620   Aesop is born.

ca. 610   Sappho, an important early Greek poet, is active.

586   The first Pythian Games are held; they will be held every four years at Delphi.

564   Solon reforms Athenian laws and makes Athens more democratic.

ca. 560   Aesop dies.

508   Cleisthenes reforms Athenian laws; Athens can now be called a democracy.

ca. 497   The Persian Wars begin.

ca. 493   Pericles, an Athenian statesman and general, is born.

490   The Athenians and Plataeans turn back a Persian invasion of Greece at the Battle of Marathon.

480   A small Greek force, led by the Spartans, holds off a much larger Persian army for a week before being destroyed at the Battle of Thermopylae.

ca. 479   The Persian Wars end.

472   Aeschylus' play *Persians*, the oldest surviving Greek play, is performed for the first time.

469   Socrates is born.

460   The First Peloponnesian War begins, with Athens and its allies fighting Sparta and its allies.

445   The First Peloponnesian War ends.

ca. 430   Herodotus' *Histories*, in which Aesop is mentioned, is written.

431   The Second Peloponnesian War begins.

ca. 429   Plato is born.

404   The Second Peloponnesian War ends with the defeat of Athens by Sparta.

ca. 400   Thucydides' *History of the Peloponnesian War* is written.

399   Socrates is executed by the Athenians after being tried and found guilty of impiety and corrupting the young.

384   Aristotle is born.

ca. 380   Plato founds the Academy, his school in Athens.
          The first written collection of *Jātaka* fables of India dates to this time; these resemble Aesop's fables in some ways.

ca. 347   Plato dies.

338   Athens loses its freedom after being defeated by the Macedonian Empire.

ca. 330   Demetrius of Phalerum compiles the earliest known collection of Aesopic fables (it has not survived).

322   Aristotle dies.

ca. 200   The first written collection of *Panchatantra* fables of India dates to this time; these share significant features with Aesop's fables.

63   The Romans capture Jerusalem.

CE

ca. 1 Phaedrus produces the oldest surviving collection of Aesopic fables in prose.

ca. 100 The earliest written version of the *Life of Aesop* is produced.

ca. 200 Babrius produces the oldest surviving collection of Aesopic fables in verse.

INTRODUCTION

AESOP'S FABLES ARE SOME OF THE OLDEST AND BEST-KNOWN STORIES in the world.[1] They have been told for thousands of years and translated into dozens of languages. Countless parents have used the fables to entertain their children while teaching them lessons about life, like telling the tale of the boy who cried wolf to get their children to tell the truth and not make up stories to get attention. But parents are not alone in recognizing the value of these stories: Aesop and the fables that carry his name have been used by some of the greatest names in Western philosophy. According to his student Plato, Socrates—often considered the founder of Western philosophy—devoted some of his final hours before his execution to putting Aesop's fables into verse. Plato's greatest student, Aristotle, explained how fables could be used in speeches for the purpose of persuading audiences (one example he gave was "The Fox and the Hedgehog," found in this book). Later, John Locke, in *Some Thoughts Concerning Education* (1693), argued that the fables should be a key component of a child's education, and even produced an edition of the fables himself. Jean-Jacques Rousseau, in his book on education *Émile* (1762), argued just as strenuously that they should *not* be part of children's education, because he felt that they were too complicated for children to understand. And the fables exert their influence even in the modern era. And more recently, the American author and cartoonist James Thurber reinterpreted them for a new audience in twentieth-century America, and in Great Britain, George Orwell used talking animals to warn of the dangers of totalitarianism in his book *Animal Farm* (1945). Authors such as David Sedaris, in *Squirrel Seeks Chipmunk* (2010), continue to use animals to tell stories today. As long as there are people to read Aesop's fables, it seems certain that these stories will endure.

Despite the tremendous popularity of his fables through the centuries, we have no certain knowledge about Aesop himself—in fact, the stories that have come to be known as "Aesop's fables" probably were not the work of a single person. The ancient texts that provide information about the fabulist are not necessarily reliable. One such source is Herodotus' *Histories*. Herodotus says that Aesop was a slave from Thrace who lived on the island of Samos and belonged to a man named Iadmon. It is a brief mention, and one that assumes that the reader has prior knowledge of Aesop as an author of fables, thereby suggesting that Aesop was already well known around 430 BCE, when Herodotus is believed to have written his work. Many people have accepted Herodotus' statement as true, but there are certainly many passages in *Histories* that we know to be incorrect, and even if Herodotus himself believed this claim to be true, he may well have been wrong. Certainly there is no unambiguous evidence to support Herodotus on this point. In addition to Herodotus' brief mention, there is a much longer work known as the *Life of Aesop*, which presents itself as a biography of Aesop.[2] The earliest known written version of this work dates to the first century CE and draws on the much older traditions that Herodotus would have known about. (There are several excerpts from the *Life* in this book; they are "The Tongues", "Aesop and His Fellow Servants", and "The Man and the Stone".) The *Life* describes Aesop as being a slave, extremely ugly and unable to speak, but also quite intelligent. One day, while working in the fields, he helps a priestess of Isis who has gotten lost. Isis rewards him with the ability not only to speak Greek but also to use the Greek language to devise clever stories, including the stories that we know as fables. When the slave overseer realizes that Aesop can speak, he worries that Aesop will report the ways in which the overseer has abused him to their master. He therefore arranges for Aesop to be sold to a slave dealer. Aesop's next master is a philosopher named Xanthus. In the subsequent, and longest, section of the *Life*, Aesop repeatedly uses his innate cleverness and the ability to speak well given to him by the gods to outwit others. Despite his education and his claims of wisdom, Xanthus is repeatedly shown to be intellectually inferior to Aesop. Although he often helps Xanthus, Aesop relentlessly pursues his own liberation and eventually succeeds in forcing Xanthus to set him free. After gaining his freedom, he travels to Babylon and, later, around the Mediterranean, lecturing to audiences for a fee. He meets his end at Delphi, home of the famous oracle, which was believed to deliver prophecies from the god Apollo. When the Delphians refuse to pay Aesop for his displays of wisdom, he insults and abuses them. Angered, they hide a golden cup from the temple in his luggage, wait for him to leave Delphi, then "find" the cup among his belongings and sentence him to death for stealing it. He tries, but fails, to persuade them to set him free, in part by telling fables. The Delphians are preparing to carry out the sentence when Aesop, preferring suicide to death at their hands, leaps from a cliff. The *Life* ends with the claim that the Delphians were later punished by the gods and by Greek armies for this crime.

The *Life of Aesop* is a dramatic and entertaining story. It has been suggested that the *Life of Aesop*, as an early example of extended prose fiction, has a role in the development of the novel. The work has also gained increasing scholarly attention in recent years, although these scholars disagree about what the *Life* is really about and how it should be read. That said, they do all agree that it is not actually a factual account of the life of an actual individual named Aesop, and that in fact "Aesop" may be as much a work of fiction as any character in the fables.[3]

As with Aesop himself, the origins of the Greek fables are lost to history. From their earliest days, the fables would have gone through a constant process of revision as they were passed from one teller to another. They began as part of a culture that relied on oral, not written, transmission, in a world where only a few people would have been able to read and write. For most people, therefore, anything they wanted to learn, keep with them, and share with others would have had to be memorized and then shared through speech. And fables, which are brief, not very detailed, and composed around vivid images—of a fox repeatedly leaping at grapes that remain just out of reach, for example—are in a perfect form for memorizing and sharing. Each fable provides a memorable example of the consequences of a particular behavior so that audiences might learn about general principles that they can apply to their own lives in particular situations. For example, it is doubtful that anyone reading this book will ever be in a tree branch listening to flattery from a fox who wants her to drop the cheese she has in her mouth—but almost everyone has been in a position where someone has tried to manipulate them with flattery. If you are in such a position and remember the fable, you can more easily recognize and resist the flatterer's attempts to seduce you into a bad decision.

Over time, as particular fables came to be recognized and appreciated for their cleverness and utility, they came to be attributed to Aesop, just as today every clever remark eventually gets attributed to Mark Twain. It may at first seem strange that the fables would be attributed to Aesop, who was supposed to have been a slave, and an ugly slave at that, instead of someone more respectable and of higher social status. But fables have long been associated with slaves because they provide a way for the weak and powerless to communicate subversive messages in a manner that is ambiguous enough to escape the notice of those with the power to punish. In their earliest form, the fables did not have the explicit moral statements that came to be attached to them later. The audience was left to determine the meaning of the fable, and this openness made it possible for the fable's author to deny any interpretation that might result in punishment. For this reason, fables have been used throughout history in a variety of times and places by those wishing to make political statements while hiding their true message from those who are unable—or unwilling—to see themselves as they are seen by the author of the fables.

In addition to their usefulness in conveying veiled messages, the fables also had practical value for slaves and others who were in positions of low status and lacked power (which may also explain why fables have long been associated with children). Many of the fables provide useful advice to such people, warning them of the importance of keeping to one's own kind ("Jupiter and the Monkey"), knowing one's limitations ("The Ox and the Frog," "The Eagle and the Crow"), and being suspicious of others ("The Cormorant and the Fishes"). Like the character of Aesop in the *Life of Aesop*, those who lack power can, with sufficient cleverness, at least sometimes overcome the powerful figures who oppress them. Aesopic fables are in this regard like the animal stories of Uncle Remus, providing some comfort to the underdogs in their struggles with the top dogs, as well as guidance as to how they can survive in a dangerous world.

Because fables leave it up to their audience to determine their meanings, it makes sense to think of fables not only as stories for children but also as a kind of philosophy that can educate us about the world and help us to think about and understand it more clearly. Saying that fables are a kind of philosophy may seem ridiculous at first. After all, we are used to thinking of fables as having a clear and simple moral lesson, which is usually explicitly stated for us at the end of the fable. This is the format used in this book. But these morals were not part of the fables as they were told in antiquity; they were added by later editors, and different editors have discovered different morals in the same fable. Take the story of the grasshopper and the ants. In this fable, the ants spend the summer gathering and storing food for the winter, while the grasshopper sings the summer away. When winter arrives, the grasshopper has no food because he has done no work, while the ants, who have worked hard, are well supplied with food. When the grasshopper comes to the ants looking for something to eat, the ants rather rudely tell him to dance and send him away, presumably to starve to death. The lesson is, to some editors, clear: "Provide today for the future" (as the book you have in your hands advises us), and this is probably the best-known moral to this fable.

But there are versions of the fable in which the grasshopper is presented as the hero, someone who wisely enjoys life while it lasts rather than spending it all in toil and drudgery as the ants do. And there are other versions where the ants and the grasshopper reconcile, throwing a party together at which the ants provide the refreshments and the grasshopper the entertainment. Which of these versions is the "best" or the "correct" one largely depends on who is reading the fable and how they choose to interpret it. Seen in the context of one set of values—the importance of thrift and hard work, and the bleak future faced by those who lack these qualities—the ants are the heroes and the grasshopper deserves to starve to death. In the context of another set of values—the ones that point out that life is too short to not take time to have fun, and that art needs no justification to exist—the grasshopper's search for joy and self-expression, even at the expense of material well-being, is the example to follow. In the context of a third set of values—the values of cooperation, diversity, and sharing—the true lesson is that everyone has different strengths and we are all happiest when we recognize that and allow everyone to make their own contributions to the group. Try it yourself: Have someone pick a few of the fables you aren't familiar with, and cover up the moral at the end of each one. Then read the fable, write your own moral (or morals), and see how close you come to the one provided. You may find that you have learned a very different lesson from the one the editors expected you to learn. That doesn't mean you are wrong, but it should give you something to think about, and in the end that is what philosophy is for: thinking, learning, and gaining wisdom as we go through life.

From slaves to philosophers, children to adults, and from ancient Greece to the modern world, Aesop's fables have provided entertainment, instruction, and food for thought. They have enduring value as stories in which a discerning reader can find much to consider and many different lessons. Hopefully you will find wisdom as well as pleasure in your reading!

Edward W. Clayton received his Ph.D. from the University of Michigan and is a Professor of Political Science at Central Michigan University in Mount Pleasant, Michigan.

THE FABLES

THE FOX AND THE STORK

A FOX ONE DAY INVITED A STORK TO DINE WITH HIM AND, WISHING to be amused at his expense, put the soup which he had for dinner in a large flat dish, so that, while he himself could lap it up quite easily, the Stork could only dip in the tips of his long bill. Some time after the Stork, bearing his treatment in mind, invited the Fox to take dinner with him. He, in his turn, put some minced meat in a long and narrow-necked vessel, into which he could easily put his bill, while Master Fox was forced to be content with licking what ran down the sides of the vessel. The Fox then remembered his old trick, and could not but admit that the Stork had well paid him out.

A joke is often returned with interest.

JUPITER AND THE CAMEL

The Camel, once upon a time, complained to Jupiter that he was not as well served as he ought to be in the means of defense and offense. "The Bull," said he, "has horns; the Boar, tusks; and the Lion and Tiger, formidable claws and fangs that make them feared and respected on all sides. I, on the other hand, have to put up with the abuse of all who choose to insult me." Jupiter angrily told him that if he would take the trouble to think, he would see that he was given qualities shared by no other Beast; and that, as a punishment for his foolish complaint, his ears should be shortened.

Individuals do not always know what is best for them.

THE WOMAN AND THE HEN

A Woman had a Hen that laid an egg every day. The Fowl was of a superior breed, and the eggs were very fine, and sold for a good price. The Woman thought that by giving the Hen twice as much food as she had been in the habit of giving, the bird might be brought to lay two eggs a day instead of one. So the quantity of food was doubled. The Hen thereupon grew very fat, and stopped laying altogether.

Figures are not always facts.

THE WOLF AND THE LAMB

A hungry Wolf one day saw a Lamb drinking at a stream below him and wished to find some excuse for eating her. "What do you mean by muddying the water I am going to drink?" said he fiercely to the Lamb. "Pray forgive me," meekly answered the Lamb; "I should be sorry in any way to displease you, but as the stream runs from you towards me, you will see that I am not to blame." "That's all very well," said the Wolf; "but you know you spoke ill of me behind my back a year ago." "Nay, believe me," replied the Lamb, "I was not then born." "It must have been your brother, then," growled the Wolf. "It cannot have been, for I never had any," answered the Lamb. "I know it was one of your lot," rejoined the Wolf, "so make no more such idle excuses." He then seized the poor Lamb, carried her off to the woods, and ate her.

The wicked always find an excuse for wrongdoing.

JUPITER AND THE BEE

A Bee made Jupiter a present of a pot of honey, which was so kindly taken that the god bade her ask what she would, and that it should be granted her. The Bee then desired that wherever she should set her sting it might wound to the death. Jupiter was loath to leave mankind at the mercy of a spiteful little insect, and was annoyed at the ill nature of her wish. He therefore said that while, for his promise's sake he would give her the power to harm, she must be careful how she used the power, for where she planted her sting she would leave it, and with it lose her life.

Evil brings evil in return.

THE WOLF, THE SHE-GOAT, AND THE KID

A She-goat, leaving her house one morning to look for food, told her Kid to bolt the door, and to open to no one who did not give as a password, "A plague on the Wolf, and all his tribe." A Wolf who was lurking about, unseen by the Goat, heard her words, and when she was gone, came and tapped at the door, and imitating her voice, said, "A plague on the Wolf, and all his tribe." He made sure that the door would be opened at once; but the Kid, whose suspicions were aroused, replied: "Show me your beard and I will let you in at once."

Double proof is surest.

THE BAT AND THE WEASELS

A Weasel seized upon a Bat, who begged hard for her life. "No, no," said the Weasel; "I give no quarter to Birds." "Birds!" cried the Bat. "I am no Bird. I am a Mouse. Look at my body." And so she got off that time. A few days after she fell into the clutches of another Weasel. The Bat cried for mercy. "No," said the Weasel; "no mercy to a Mouse."

"But," said the Bat, "you can see from my wings that I am a Bird." And she escaped that time as well.

It is good to have two strings to one's bow.

THE LION'S SHARE

The Lion and several other Beasts once agreed to live peaceably together in the forest, sharing equally all the spoils of hunting. One day, a fine fat Stag fell into a snare set by the Goat, who thereupon called the rest together. The Lion divided the Stag into four parts. Taking the best piece for himself, he said, "This is mine, of course, as I am the Lion." Taking another portion, he added, "This too is mine by right—the right, if you must know, of the strongest." Further, putting aside the third piece, "That's for the most valiant," said he; "and as for the remaining part, touch it if you dare."

Might makes right.

THE ASS, THE APE, AND THE MOLE

An Ass and an Ape were one day grumbling together over their grievances. "My ears are so long that people laugh at me," said the Ass; "I wish I had horns like the Ox." "And I," said the Ape, "am really ashamed to turn my back upon anyone. Why should not I have a fine bushy tail as well as that saucy fellow the Fox?" "Hold your tongues, both of you," said a Mole that overheard them, "and be thankful for what you have. The poor Moles have no horns at all, no tail to speak of, and are nearly blind as well."

We should never complain so long as there are
others worse off than ourselves.

THE LION, THE TIGER, AND THE FOX

A Lion and a Tiger happened to come together over the dead body of a Fawn that had been recently shot. A fierce battle ensued, and as each animal was in the prime of his age and strength, the combat was long and furious. At last they lay stretched on the ground panting, bleeding, and exhausted, each unable to lift a paw against the other. An impudent Fox coming by at the time stepped in and carried off before their eyes the prey on account of which they had both fought so savagely. "Woe betide us," said the Lion, "that we should suffer so much to serve a Fox!"

It often happens that one has the toil and another the profit.

THE FIGHTING COCKS

Two Cocks fought for the sovereignty of the farmyard. One was severely beaten, and ran and hid himself in a hole. The conqueror flew to the top of an outhouse, there clapped his wings, and crowed out "Victory!" Just then an Eagle made a swoop, seized him, and carried him off. The other, seeing this from his hiding-place, came out, and, shaking off the recollection of his late disgrace, strutted about among his Hens with all the dignity imaginable.

Bear success with moderation.

THE CAT AND THE MICE

A certain house was much infested by Mice. The owner brought home a Cat, a famous mouser, who soon made such havoc among the little folk that those who were left stayed closely in the upper shelves. Then the Cat grew hungry and thin, and, driven to her wit's end, hung by her hind legs from a peg in the wall, and pretended to be dead, in order that the Mice would no longer be afraid to come near her. An

The Lion, the Tiger, and the Fox

old Mouse came to the edge of the shelf, and, seeing through the trick, cried out, "Ah, ha, Mrs. Pussy! We should not come near you, even if your skin were stuffed with straw."

Old birds are not to be caught with chaff.

THE PEACOCK'S COMPLAINT

The Peacock complained to Juno that while everyone laughed at his voice, an insignificant creature like the Nightingale had a note that delighted all listeners. Juno, angry at the unreasonableness of her favorite bird, scolded him in the following terms: "Envious bird that you are, I am sure you have no cause to complain. On your neck shine all the colors of the rainbow, and your extended tail gleams like a mass of gems. No living being has every good thing to its own share. The Falcon is endowed with swiftness; the Eagle, strength; the Parrot, speech; the Raven, the gift of augury; and the Nightingale, a melodious note; while you have both size and beauty. Cease then to complain, or the gifts you have shall be taken away."

Contentment should be the source of every joy.

THE TWO FROGS

Two Frogs lived in the same pool. The hot summer came and dried it up, so that they were forced to set forth in search of other water. As they went along they chanced to find a deep well full of cool water. "Let us jump in here!" cried one of the Frogs. "Wait a bit," said the other; "if that should dry up, how could we get out again?"

Easier in than out.

THE TWO CRABS

"My dear," called out an old Crab to her daughter one day, "why do you sidle along in that awkward manner? Why don't you go forward like other people?" "Well, mother," answered the young Crab, "it seems to me that I go exactly like you do. Go first and show me how, and I will gladly follow."

Example is better than precept.

THE COUNTRYMAN AND THE SNAKE

A Countryman, one frosty day in the depth of winter, found a Snake under a hedge almost dead with the cold. Taking pity on the poor creature, he brought it home, and laid it on the hearth near the fire. Revived by the heat, it reared itself up, and with dreadful hissings flew at the wife and children of its benefactor. The Countryman, hearing their cries, rushed in, and, seizing a mattock, soon cut the Snake in pieces. "Vile wretch!" said he; "is this the reward you make to him who saved your life? Die, as you deserve; but a single death is too good for you."

Ingratitude is a crime.

THE KITE AND THE PIGEONS

A Kite that had kept sailing around a dovecote looking for a nice fat Pigeon for many days, to no purpose, was forced by hunger to have recourse to stratagem. Approaching the Pigeons in his gentlest manner, he tried to show them how much better their state would be if they had a king with some firmness about him, and how well his protection would shield them from the attacks of the Hawk and other enemies. The Pigeons, deluded by this show of reason, admitted him to the dovecote as their king. They found, however, that he thought it part of his kingly prerogative to eat one of their number every day, and they soon repented of their credulity in having let him in. "Ah!" they exclaimed in despair; "we deserve no better. Why did we heed the counsel of an enemy?"

Trust not your security to one who puts his own interests first.

THE BODY AND ITS MEMBERS[1]

The members of the Body once rebelled against him. They said he led an idle, lazy life at their expense. The Hands declared that they would not again lift a crust even to keep him from starving, the Mouth that it would not take in a bit more food, the Legs that they would carry him about no longer, and so on with the others. The Body quietly allowed them to follow their own courses, well knowing that they would all soon come to their senses, as indeed they did, when, for want of the blood and nourishment supplied from the stomach, they found themselves fast becoming mere skin and bone.

No one can live to himself, but must take account of his neighbors' needs.

THE SPENDTHRIFT AND THE SWALLOW

A prodigal young Fellow, who had run through all his money and even sold all his outer clothes except his cloak, saw a Swallow skimming over the meadows one fine day in the early spring. Believing that summer was really come, he sold his cloak too. The next morning there happened to be a severe frost, and, shivering and nearly frozen himself, he found the Swallow lying stiff and dead upon the ground. He thereupon upbraided the poor bird as the cause of all his misfortunes. "Stupid thing!" said he, "had you not come before your time, I should not now be so wretched."

Be not ready to believe rumors.

The Hawk and the Nightingale

THE HAWK AND THE NIGHTINGALE

A Nightingale once fell into the clutches of a hungry Hawk who had been all day on the lookout for food. "Pray let me go," said the Nightingale, "I am such a mite for a stomach like yours. I sing so nicely, too. Do let me go, it will do you good to hear me." "Much good it will do an empty stomach," replied the Hawk, "and besides, a little bird that I have is more to me than a great one that has yet to be caught."

A bird in the hand is worth two in the bush.

THE STAG AT THE POOL

A Stag, drinking at a clear pool, admired the handsome look of his spreading antlers, but was much displeased at the slim and ungainly appearance of his legs. "What a glorious pair of branching horns!" said he. "How gracefully they hang over my forehead! What a fine air they give my face! But as for my spindle-shanks of legs, I am heartily ashamed of them." The words were scarcely out of his mouth when he saw some huntsmen and a pack of hounds making towards him. His despised legs soon placed him at a distance from his followers but, on entering the forest, his horns got entangled at every turn, so that the dogs soon reached him and made an end of him. "Fool that I was!" he gasped at his last breath; "had it not been for these wretched horns, my legs would have saved my life."

Beauty may have fair leaves and bitter fruit.

THE BROTHER AND SISTER

A certain Man had two children, a boy and a girl. The lad was a handsome young fellow, but the girl was as plain as a girl can well be. The Sister, provoked beyond endurance by the way in which her

Brother looked in the glass and made remarks to her disadvantage, went to her father and complained of it. The father drew his children to him very tenderly, and said, "My dears, I wish you both to look in the glass every day. You, my son, seeing your face is handsome, may take care not to spoil it by ill-temper and bad behavior; and you, my daughter, may be encouraged to make up for your want of beauty by the sweetness of your manners, and the grace of your conversation."

Handsome is as handsome does.

THE MAN AND HIS TWO WIVES

In a country where Men could have more than one Wife, a certain Man, whose head was fast becoming white, had two, one a little older than himself, and one much younger. The young Wife, being of a gay and lively turn, did not want people to think that she had an old man for a husband, and so used to pull out as many of his white hairs as she could. The old Wife, on the other hand, did not wish to seem older than her husband, and so used to pull out the black hairs. This went on, until between them both, they made the poor Man quite bald.

No man can belong to two parties at once.

THE MISCHIEVOUS DOG

A rascally Dog used to run quietly to the heels of every passerby, and bite them without warning. So his master was obliged to tie a bell around the cur's neck that he might give notice wherever he went. This the Dog thought very fine indeed, and he went about tinkling it in pride all over town. But an old Hound said: "Why do you make such a fool of yourself? That bell is not a mark of merit, but of disgrace."

Notoriety is often mistaken for fame.

THE FROGS AND THE FIGHTING BULLS

A Frog, one day peeping out of a marsh, saw two Bulls fighting at some distance off in the meadow. "Alas! My friends," cried he to his fellow Frogs, "whatever will become of us?" "Why, what are you frightened at?" asked one of the Frogs; "what can their quarrels have to do with us? They are only proving which shall be master of the herd." "True," answered the first, "and it is just that which causes my fear, for the one that is beaten will take refuge here in the marshes, and will tread us to death." And so it happened; and many a Frog, in dying, had sore proof that the fears which he had thought to be groundless were not so in fact.

Coming events often cast their shadows before.

THE OX AND THE FROG

An Ox grazing in a meadow chanced to set his foot on a young Frog and crushed him to death. His brothers and sisters, who were playing near, at once ran to tell their mother what had happened. "The monster that did it, mother, was such a size!" said they. The mother, who was a vain old thing, thought that she could easily make herself as large. "Was it as big as this?" she asked, blowing and puffing herself out. "Oh, much bigger than that!" replied the young Frogs. "As this, then?" cried she, puffing and blowing again with all her might. "Nay, mother," said they; "if you were to try till you burst yourself, you would never be so big." The silly old Frog tried to puff herself out still more, and burst herself indeed.

People are ruined by attempting a greatness to which they have no claim.

THE COLLIER AND THE FULLER[2]

A friendly Collier meeting one day with a Fuller, an old acquaintance of his, kindly invited him to come and share his house. "A thousand thanks for your civility," replied the Fuller; "but I am rather afraid that as fast as I make anything clean, you will be smutting it again."

Good conduct is often corrupted by false knowledge.

THE MAN AND THE LION

A Man and a Lion once argued together as to which belonged to the nobler race. The Man called the attention of the Lion to a monument on which was sculptured a Man striding over a fallen Lion. "That proves nothing at all," said the Lion; "if a Lion had been the carver, he would have made the Lion striding over the Man."

Men are but sorry witnesses in their own cause.

THE ANT AND THE FLY

An Ant and a Fly one day disputed as to their respective merits. "Vile creeping insect!" said the Fly to the Ant, "can you for a moment compare yourself with me? I soar on the wing like a bird. I enter the palaces of kings, and alight on the heads of princes, nay, of emperors, and only quit them to adorn the yet more attractive brow of beauty. Besides, I visit the altars of the gods. Not a sacrifice is offered but is first tasted by me. Every feast, too, is open to me. I eat and drink of the best, instead of living for days on two or three grains of corn as you do." "All that's very fine," replied the Ant; "but listen to me. You boast of your feasting, but you know that your diet is not always so choice, and you are sometimes forced to eat what nothing should induce me to touch. As for alighting on the heads of kings and emperors, you know very well that whether you pitch on the head of an emperor, or of an ass (and it is as often on the one as the other), you are shaken off from both with impatience. And, then, the 'altars of the gods,' indeed! There and everywhere else you are looked upon as nothing but a nuisance. In the winter, too, while I feed at my ease on the fruit of my toil, I often see your friends dying with cold, hunger, and fatigue. I lose my time now in talking to you. Chattering will fill neither my bin nor my cupboard."

Bread earned by toil is sweet.

THE STAG IN THE OX-STALL

A Stag, hard pressed by the Hounds, ran for shelter into an ox-stall, the door of which was open. One of the Oxen turned round, and asked him why he came to such a place as that, where he would be sure to be taken. The Stag replied that he should do well enough if the Oxen would not tell of him; and, covering himself in a heap of straw, waited for the night. Several servants, and even the Overseer himself, came and looked round, but saw nothing of the Stag, who, as each went away, was ready to jump out of his skin for joy, and warmly thanked the Oxen for their silence. The Ox who had spoken first to him warned him not to be too sure of his escape, and said that, glad as they would all be for him to get away, there was a certain person still to come whose eyes were a deal sharper than the eyes of anyone who had been there yet. This was the Master himself, who, having been dining with a neighbor, looked in on his way home to see that all was right. At a glance he saw the tips of the horns coming through the straw, whereupon he raised a hue and cry, called all his people together, and made a prize of the Stag.

The eye of the master does more than all his servants.

THE BOASTING TRAVELER

A Man was one day entertaining a lot of fellows with an account of the wonders he had done when abroad on his travels. "I was once at Rhodes," said he, "and the people of Rhodes, you know, are famous for jumping. Well, I took a jump there that no other man could come within a yard of. That's a fact, and if we were there I could bring you ten men who would prove it." "What need is there to go to Rhodes for witnesses?" asked one of his hearers; "just imagine that you are there now, and show us your leap."

Seeing is believing.

THE BALD KNIGHT

A certain Knight, who wore a wig to conceal his baldness, was out hunting one day. A sudden gust of wind carried away his wig, and showed his bald pate. His friends all laughed heartily at the odd figure he made, but the old fellow, so far from being put out, laughed as heartily as any of them. "Is it any wonder," said he, "that another man's hair shouldn't keep on my head when my own wouldn't stay there?"

Every event has its reason.

THE LIONESS AND THE FOX

The Fox once observed to the Lioness that Foxes were very much to be envied in the matter of fruitfulness. Scarcely a year passed that she, for instance, did not bring into the world a good litter of cubs, while some who had young only one at a time, and that not more than twice or thrice in their lives, looked down upon everybody else with contempt. This sneer was too pointed to be passed over in silence by the Lioness, who replied with a good deal of fire, "What you say is true. You have a great many children; but what are they? Foxes. I have only one, but remember that it is a Lion."

Prefer quality to quantity.

THE LEOPARD AND THE FOX

The Leopard one day, in the hearing of the Fox, was very loud in the praise of his own beautifully spotted skin. The Fox thereupon told him that, handsome as he might be, he considered that he himself was yet a great deal handsomer. "Your beauty is of the body," said the Fox; "mine is of the mind."

Beauty is skin deep.

THE WANTON CALF

A Calf full of play and wantonness, seeing an Ox at the plow, could not forbear insulting him. "What a sorry old drudge you are," said he, "to bear that heavy yoke upon your neck, and with a plow at your tail all day, to go turning up the ground for a master. You are a wretched slave, and know no better, or you would not do it. See what a happy life I lead; I go just where I please—sometimes in the cool shade, sometimes in the warm sunshine; and whenever I like, I drink at the clear, running brook." The Ox, not at all moved by this address, went on quietly and calmly with his work, and in the evening, when unyoked and going to take his rest, he saw the Calf being led off by the butcher. He pitied him, but could not help saying, as he passed, "Now, friend, whose condition is the better, yours or mine?"

Youth and folly often live together.

THE LION AND THE MOUSE

A Lion, tired with the chase, lay sleeping at full length under a shady tree. Some Mice scrambling over him while he slept, awoke him. Laying his paw upon one of them, he was about to crush him, when the Mouse implored his mercy. "Spare me, O King!" said he, "and maybe the day will come when I can be of service to you." The Lion, tickled with the idea of the Mouse helping him, lifted his paw and let the little

The Lion and the Mouse

creature go. Some time after, the Lion was caught in a net laid by some hunters, and, unable to free himself, made the forest resound with his roars. The Mouse whose life had been spared came, and with his little sharp teeth soon gnawed the ropes asunder, and set the Lion free.

The least may help the greatest.

THE FATAL COURTSHIP

The freed Lion spoken of in the last fable was so grateful to the Mouse that he told him to name what he most desired, and he should have his wish. The Mouse, fired with ambition, said, "I desire the hand of your daughter in marriage." This the Lion good-naturedly gave him, and called the young Lioness to come that way. She did so; and rushed up so heedlessly that she did not see her small suitor, but placed her paw on him and crushed him to death.

Bad wishing makes bad getting.

THE SICK KITE

A Kite who had been ill for a long time begged of his mother to go to all the temples in the country, and see what prayers and promises could do for his recovery. The old Kite replied, "My son, unless you can think of an altar that neither of us has robbed, I fear that nothing can be done for you in that way."

Be in health what you wish to be when you are ill.

THE JACKDAW AND THE PIGEONS

A Jackdaw, seeing how well some Pigeons in a certain dovecote fed and how happily they lived together, wished much to join them. With this view he whitened his feathers, and slipped in one evening just as it was getting dark. As long as he kept quiet he escaped notice, but growing bolder by degrees, and feeling very jolly in his new quarters, he burst into a hearty laugh. His voice betrayed him. The Pigeons set upon him and drove him out. When he would afterwards have joined the Jackdaws again, his discolored feathers and his battered state drew attention to him, and his former mates, finding out what he had been at, would let him have no further part with them.

He who pursues two courses succeeds with neither.

THE EAGLE, THE CAT, AND THE SOW

An Eagle had built her nest in the top branches of an old oak tree; a wild Cat dwelt in a hole about the middle; and in the hollow part at the bottom lived a Sow with a whole litter of pigs. They might have remained there long in contentment, but the Cat, bent upon mischief, climbed up one day to the Eagle, and said, "Neighbor, have you noticed what the old Sow who lives below is doing? I believe she is determined upon nothing less than to root up this tree, our abode, and when it falls she will devour our young ones." This put the Eagle in a great fright, and she did not dare to stir from home lest the tree might fall in her absence. Creeping down to visit the Sow, the wily Cat said, "Listen to me, my friend. Last night I overheard that old Bird who lives over our heads promise her young ones that the very next time you went out they should have one of your dear little porkers for supper." The Sow, greatly alarmed in her turn, dared not quit her hollow. The mutual fear of the Eagle and the Sow became so great that they and their young ones were actually starved to death, and fell a prey to the designing old Cat and her kittens.

Too much belief is worse than too little.

THE HARES AND THE FROGS

The Hares once took serious counsel among themselves whether death itself would not be better than their wretched lot. "What a sad state is ours," they said, "never to eat in comfort, always to sleep in fear, to be startled by a shadow, and fly with beating heart at the rustling of the leaves. Better death by far"; and off they went accordingly to drown themselves in a neighboring lake. Some scores of Frogs who were enjoying the moonlight on the bank, scared at the approach of the Hares, jumped into the water. The splash awoke fresh fears in the breasts of the timid Hares, and they came to a full stop in their flight. One wise old fellow among them cried, "Hold, brothers! See, weak and fearful as we are, beings exist that are more weak and fearful still! Why then should we seek to die? Let us rather make the best of our lot, such as it is."

There are always some whose station is worse than your own.

―――――――――

THE WOLF AND THE CRANE

A Wolf one day ate his food so greedily that a bone stuck in his throat, giving him great pain. He ran howling up and down, and offered to reward handsomely anyone who would pull it out. A Crane, moved by pity as well as by the prospect of the money, undertook the dangerous task. Having removed the bone, he asked for the promised reward. "Reward!" cried the Wolf; "pray, you greedy fellow, what reward can you possibly require? You have had your head in my mouth, and instead of biting it off, I have let you pull it out unharmed. Get away with you, and don't come again within reach of my paw."

Know those whom you would serve.

―――――――――

THE FOX AND THE GOAT

A Fox once fell into a well, and tried vainly for a long time to get out again. At last a foolish Goat came by and asked the Fox if the water were good. "Splendid!" said the wily Fox. "It is so fine that I cannot get enough of it." The Goat eagerly leaped in, when the Fox, taking

The Wolf and the Crane

advantage of the other's horns, climbed out to safety. "If you had half as much brain as beard," said the Fox as he sneaked away, "you would have bethought yourself how to get out, before you got in."

Use a man as he deserves.

THE LION IN LOVE

A Lion once fell in love with the fair daughter of a Forester, and demanded her of her father in marriage. The Man dared not refuse, though he would gladly have done so; but he told the suitor that his daughter was so young and delicate, he could consent only after the Lion's teeth were drawn and his claws cut off. The Lion was so enslaved by love that he agreed to this without a murmur, and it was accordingly done. The Forester then seized a club, laid him dead upon the spot, and so broke off the match.

Foolish love brings sorrow.

THE DOG AND HIS SHADOW

A Dog, bearing in his mouth a piece of meat that he had stolen, was crossing a smooth stream by means of a plank. Looking in, he saw what he took to be another dog carrying another piece of meat. Snapping greedily to get this as well, he let go the meat that he had, and lost it in the stream.

Catch at the shadow and you lose the substance.

THE GENEROUS LION

A Lion, having slain a Bullock, stood over it, lashing his sides with his tail. A Thief who was passing by stopped and impudently demanded half shares. "You are always too ready to take what does not belong to you," answered the Lion; "go your way, I have nothing to say to you." The Thief saw that the Lion was not to be trifled with, and went off. Just then a Traveler came up, and seeing the Lion, modestly withdrew. The generous Beast, with a courteous air, called him forward, and, dividing the Bullock in halves, told the Man to take one, and in order that the latter might be under no restraint, carried his own portion away into the forest.

Modesty gains favor in a king's eyes.

THE LION, THE ASS, AND THE FOX

The Lion, the Ass, and the Fox went hunting together, and it was agreed that whatever was taken should be shared among them. They caught a large fat Stag, which the Lion ordered the Ass to divide. The Ass took a deal of pains to divide the Stag into three pieces, which should be as nearly equal as possible. The Lion, enraged with him for what he considered a want of proper respect to his quality, flew upon him and tore him to pieces. He then called on the Fox to divide. The Fox, nibbling off a small portion for himself, left the rest for the Lion's share. The Lion, highly pleased with this mark of respect, asked the Fox where he had learned such politeness and good-breeding. "To tell the truth, Sire," replied the Fox, "I was taught it by the Ass that lies dead there."

Better to learn by the misfortunes of others than by your own.

CÆSAR AND THE SLAVE

During a visit that Tiberius Cæsar[3] paid to one of his country residences he observed that, whenever he walked in the grounds, a certain Slave was always a little way ahead of him, busily watering the paths. Turn which way he would, go where he might, there was the fellow still fussing about with his watering-pot. He felt sure that he was making himself thus needlessly officious in the hope of thereby gaining his liberty. In making a Slave free, a part of the ceremony consisted in giving him a gentle stroke on one side of the face. Hence, when the man came running up in eager expectation, at the call of the Emperor, the latter said to him, "I have for a long time observed you meddling where you had nothing to do, and while you might have been better employed elsewhere. You are mistaken if you think I can afford a box on the ear at so low a price as you bid for it."

Being busy does not always mean being useful.

THE FOX AND THE SICK LION

It was reported that the Lion was sick and confined to his den, where he would be happy to see any of his subjects who might come to pay the homage that was due to him. Many accordingly went in, and fell an easy prey to the old Lion, who devoured them at his leisure. But it was observed that the Fox very carefully kept away. The Lion noticed his absence, and sent one of his Jackals to express a hope that he would show he was not insensible to motives of respect and charity, by coming and paying his duty like the rest. The Fox told the Jackal to offer his sincerest reverence to his master, and to say that he had more than once been on the point of coming to see him. "But the truth of the matter," he observed dryly, "is that all the footprints I see go into the cave, but none come out again. So for the present my health demands that I stay away."

It is wise to see one's way out before one ventures in.

THE TORTOISE AND THE EAGLE

A Tortoise, weary of crawling about on the ground at a snail's pace, desired to fly in the air like the Birds, and gave out that if any Bird would take him up in the clouds and show him the world, he would tell him in return where to find treasures hid in the earth. The Eagle thereupon did as he wished, but finding that the Tortoise could not keep his word, carried him up once more, and let him fall on a hard rock, where he was dashed to pieces.

Never make rash promises.

THE ASS AND THE LITTLE DOG

The Ass, observing how great a favorite a Little Dog was with his Master—how much caressed, and fondled, and fed with choice bits at every meal, and for no other reason that he could see, but skipping and frisking about and wagging his tail—resolved to imitate him, and see whether the same behavior would not bring him similar favors. Accordingly, the Master was no sooner come home from walking, and seated in his easy-chair, than the Ass came into the room, and danced around him with many an awkward gambol. The Man could not help laughing aloud at the odd sight. The joke, however, became serious, when the Ass, rising on his hind-legs, laid his forefeet upon his Master's shoulders, and braying in his face in the most fascinating manner, would fain have jumped into his lap. The Man cried out for help, and one of his servants running in with a good stick, laid it unmercifully on the bones of the poor Ass, who was glad to get back to his stable.

A place for everyone, and everyone in his place.

THE FOX AND THE BRAMBLE

A Fox, hotly pursued by the Hounds, jumped through a hedge, and his feet were sadly torn by a Bramble that grew in its midst. He fell to licking his paws, with many a curse against the Bramble for its unkind treatment. "Softly, softly, good words if you please, Master Fox," said the Bramble. "I thought you knew better than to lay hold of one whose nature it is to lay hold of others."

Never trust the untrustworthy.

THE FOX WITHOUT A TAIL

A Fox was once caught in a trap by his tail, and in order to get away was forced to leave it behind. Knowing that without a tail he would be a laughingstock for all his fellows, he resolved to try to induce them to part with theirs. So at the next assembly of Foxes he made a speech on the unprofitableness of tails in general, and the inconvenience of a Fox's tail in particular, adding that he had never felt so easy as since he had given up his own. When he had sat down, a sly old fellow rose, and waving his long brush with a graceful air, said, with a sneer, that if, like the last speaker, he had lost his tail, nothing further would have been needed to convince him; but till such an accident should happen, he should certainly vote in favor of tails.

Guard against those who would wish you to be reduced to their own level.

THE WIND AND THE SUN

A dispute once arose between the North Wind and the Sun as to which was the stronger of the two. Seeing a Traveler on his way, they agreed to see which could the sooner get his cloak off him. The North Wind began, and sent a furious blast, which, at the onset, nearly tore the cloak from its fastenings; but the Traveler, seizing the garment with a firm grip, held it round his body so tightly that the North Wind spent his remaining force in vain. The Sun, dispelling the clouds that had gathered, then darted his genial beams on the Traveler's head. Growing faint with the heat, the Man flung off his coat, and ran for protection to the nearest shade.

Mildness governs more than anger.

The Fox without a Tail

THE GOOSE THAT LAID THE GOLDEN EGGS

A certain Man had a Goose that laid him a golden egg every day. Being of a covetous turn, he thought if he killed his Goose he should come at once to the source of his treasure. So he killed her, and cut her open, when great was his dismay to find that her inside was in no way different from that of any other Goose.

Greediness overreaches itself.

THE WOLF, THE FOX, AND THE APE

The Wolf charged the Fox, before the Ape as judge, with having stolen some meat that he had put by. The case was long and angrily contested, and the Ape, having heard all that was to be said on both sides, announced his decision as follows: "You, Master Wolf, in spite of your complaints, do not appear to me to have had anything to lose; but I am forced to admit that you, Master Fox, have certainly stolen what is laid to your charge."

The dishonest get no credit.

THE THIEF AND HIS MOTHER

A little Boy who went to school stole one of his schoolfellow's books and took it home. His Mother, so far from correcting him, took the book and sold it, and gave him an apple for his pains. In the course of time the Boy became a Thief, and at last was tried for his life and condemned. He was led to the gallows, a great crowd of people following, and among them his Mother, weeping bitterly. Seeing her, he prayed the officers to grant him the favor of a few parting words with her, and his request was freely granted. He went to his Mother, put his arm round her neck, and making as though he would whisper something in her ear, bit it off. Her cry of pain drew everybody's eyes upon them, and great was the indignation, that at such a time he should add another violence to his list of crimes. "Nay, good people," said he, "do not be deceived. My first theft was of a book, which I gave to my Mother. Had she whipped me for it, instead of praising me, I should not have come to the gallows now that I am a man."

Spare the rod, spoil the child.

THE TWO POTS

A River having overflowed its banks, two Pots were carried along in the stream, one made of Earthenware and the other of Brass. "Well, brother, since we share the same fate, let us go along together," cried the Brazen Pot (who before that had been haughty enough) to the Earthen one. "No, no!" replied the latter in a great fright; "keep off, whatever you do, for if you knock against me, or I against you, it will be all over with me—to the bottom I shall go."

Equals make the best friends.

THE FARMER AND THE STORK

A Farmer set a net in his fields to catch the Cranes and Geese which came to feed upon the newly springing corn. He took several, and with them a Stork, who pleaded hard for his life on the ground that he was neither a Goose nor a Crane, but a poor harmless Stork. "That may be very true," replied the Man; "but as I have taken you in bad company, you must expect to suffer the same punishment."

Evil company proves more than fair professions.

THE GOAT AND THE BOY

A Boy whose business it was to look after some Goats gathered them together as night began to fall to lead them home. One of the number refused to obey his call, and stood on a ledge of a rock, nibbling the herbage that grew there. The Boy lost all patience, and taking up a stone, threw it at the Goat with all his might. The stone struck one of the horns of the Goat, and broke it off at the middle. The Boy, terrified at what he had done and fearing his master's anger, threw himself upon his knees before the Goat, and begged her to say nothing to the master about the mishap, as it was far from his intention to aim the stone so well. "Tush!" replied the Goat. "Let my tongue be ever so silent, my horn is sure to tell the tale."

Do not attempt to hide what cannot be hid.

THE MAN AND THE WEASEL

A man caught a Weasel and was about to kill it. The little animal prayed earnestly for his life. "You will not be so unkind," said he to the Man, "as to slay a poor creature who kills your Mice for you?" "For me!" answered the Man; "that's a good joke. For me, you say, as if you did not catch them more for your own pleasure than for my profit. And as to making away with my food, you know that you do as much harm as the Mice themselves. You must make some better excuse than that, before I shall feel inclined to spare you." Having said this, he strangled the Weasel without more ado.

A poor excuse is a dangerous thing.

THE SHEEP-BITER

A certain Shepherd had a Dog in whom he placed such great trust that he would often leave the flock to his sole care. As soon as his Master's back was turned, however, the Cur, although well fed and kindly treated, used to worry the Sheep, and would sometimes kill one and devour a portion. The Man at last found out how much his confidence had been abused, and resolved to hang the Dog without mercy. When the rope was put around his neck, the Dog pleaded hard for his life, and begged his Master rather to hang the Wolf, who had done ten times as much harm to the flock as he had. "That may be," replied the Man sternly; "but you are ten times the greater villain for all that. Nothing shall save you from the fate which your treachery deserves."

The most dangerous enemy is the one within.

FORTUNE AND THE BOY

A Little Boy, quite tired out with play, stretched out, and fell sound asleep close to the edge of a deep well. Fortune came by and, gently waking him said, "My dear Boy, believe me, I have saved your life. If you had fallen in, everybody would have laid the blame on me; but tell me truly, now, would the fault have been yours or mine?"

Lay the blame where it belongs.

DEATH AND CUPID

One sultry summer's noon, tired with play and faint with heat, Cupid went into a cool grotto to repose himself. This happened to be the cave of Death. He threw himself carelessly down upon the floor, and his quiver turning upside down, all the arrows fell out, and mingled with those of Death, which lay scattered about the place. When he awoke, he gathered them up as well as he could; but they were so intermingled that, although he knew the proper number to take, he could not rightly distinguish his own. Hence he took up some of the arrows that belonged to Death, and left some of his. This is the reason why we now and then see the hearts of the old and decrepit transfixed with the bolts of Love; and with great grief and surprise, sometimes see youth and beauty smitten with the darts of Death.

Death and Love strike unexpectedly.

THE TRAVELERS AND THE BEAR

Two Men about to journey through a forest agreed to stand by each other in any dangers that might befall. They had not gone far before a savage Bear rushed out from a thicket and stood in their path. One of the Travelers, a light, nimble fellow, got up into a tree. The other, seeing that there was no chance to defend himself singlehanded, fell flat on his face and held his breath. The Bear came up and smelled at him, and taking him for dead, went off again into the wood. The Man in the tree came down and, rejoining his companion, asked him, with a sly smile, what was the wonderful secret which he had seen the Bear whisper into his ear. "Why," replied the other, "he told me to take care for the future and not to put any confidence in such cowardly rascals as you."

Trust not fine promises.

THE VIPER AND THE FILE

A Viper entered a smith's shop and looked up and down for something to eat. He settled at last upon a File, and began to gnaw it greedily. "Bite away," said the File gruffly, "you'll get little from me. It is my business to take from all and give to none."

Before you attack, know thine enemy.

THE BULL AND THE GOAT

A Bull, being pursued by a Lion, spied a cave and fled towards it, meaning to take shelter there. A Goat came to the mouth of the cave, and, menacing the Bull with his horns, disputed the passage. The Bull, having no time to lose, was obliged to make off again without delay, but not before saying to the Goat, "Were it not for the Lion that is behind me, I would soon let you know the difference between a Bull and a Goat."

Valor does not always show itself in blows.

The Travelers and the Bear

THE DOG IN THE MANGER

A Dog was lying in a Manger full of hay. An Ox, being hungry, came near and was going to eat of the hay. The Dog, getting up and snarling at him, would not let him touch it. "Surly creature," said the Ox, "you cannot eat the hay yourself, and yet you will let no one else have any."

Do not begrudge others what you yourself cannot enjoy.

THE FOX AND THE MASK

A Fox was one day rummaging in the house of an actor, and came across a very beautiful Mask. Putting his paw on the forehead, he said, "What a handsome face we have here! It is a pity that it should want brains."

Beauty without brains nothing gains.

THE STAG AND THE FAWN

A Fawn once said to a Stag, "How is it that you, who are so much bigger, and stronger, and fleeter than a Dog, are in such a fright when you behold one? If you stood your ground, and used your horns, I should think the Hounds would fly from you." "I have said that to myself, little one, over and over again," replied the Stag, "and made up my mind to act upon it; but yet, no sooner do I hear the voice of a Dog than I am ready to jump out of my skin."

No arguments will give courage to a coward.

THE RIVER FISH AND THE SEA FISH

A large freshwater Pike was carried out to sea by a strong current. He gave himself great airs on account of what he considered his superior race and descent, and despised the Sea Fishes among whom he found himself. "You value yourself at a great price," said a little stranger, "but if ever it is our fate to come to the market, you will find that I am thought a good deal more of there than you."

Size does not determine value.

THE MAN AND THE TREES

One day a Man went into a Forest and asked the Trees if they would be so good as to give him a handle for his axe. The Trees readily granted his request and gave him a piece of tough Ash. But no sooner had the Man fitted it into his axe head, than he quickly began to use it, and laid about him so vigorously that the giants of the Forest fell under his strokes. "Alas!"said a doomed Oak to a Cedar, "the first step lost us all. If we had not given up our rights to the Ash, we might have stood for ages."

Let not your conduct furnish a handle against yourself.

THE ASS, THE LION, AND THE COCK

An Ass and a Cock, feeding in the same meadow, were one day surprised by a Lion. The Cock crowed loudly, and the Lion (who is said to have a great antipathy to the crowing of a Cock) at once turned tail and ran off again. The Ass, believing that it was from fear of him that the Lion fled, pursued him. As soon as they were out of hearing of the Cock, the Lion turned round upon the Ass and tore him in pieces.

False confidence leads one to danger.

THE HART AND THE VINE

A Hart, being hard pursued by the hunters, hid himself under the broad leaves of a shady, spreading Vine. When the hunters had gone by and given him over for lost, he thought himself quite secure, and began to crop and eat the leaves of the Vine. The rustling of the branches drew the eyes of the hunters that way, and they shot their arrows there at a venture, and killed the Hart. "I am rightly served," gasped he in dying, "for I ought not to have mistreated the friend who would have saved me."

Be not forgetful of benefits.

THE VAIN JACKDAW

A discontented Jackdaw once found some feathers which had fallen from the Peacocks, and dressed himself with his picked-up plumage. Then he sought out the company of these Birds, and strutted about with them, much pleased with his looks. But they soon found him out, pulled their feathers off him, and treated him so roughly that he was glad to flee from them. He went back to the society of his fellow Jackdaws, but they in turn would have nothing to do with so sorry looking a bird.

The honest man shuns pretension.

THE OAK AND THE REEDS

A violent storm uprooted an Oak that grew on the bank of a river. The Oak drifted across the stream and lodged among some Reeds. Wondering to find these still standing, he could not help asking them how it was they had escaped the fury of a storm which had torn him up by the roots. "We bent our heads to the blast," said they, "and it passed over us. You stood stiff and stubborn till you could stand no longer."

Stoop to conquer.

THE MISER

A Miser once buried all his money in the earth, at the foot of a tree, and went every day to feast upon the sight of his treasure. A thievish fellow, who had watched him at this occupation, came one night and carried off the gold. The next day the Miser, finding his treasure gone, tore his clothes and filled the air with his lamentations. A neighbor hearing his outcry and learning the cause said, "Pray do not grieve so; but go and get a stone, place it in the hole, and fancy it is your gold. It will be of quite as much service as the money was."

Nothing is of value that is not of use.

THE FLYING-FISH AND THE DOLPHIN

A Flying-Fish, being pursued by a Dolphin, swam for safety into shallow water. Seeing the Dolphin still after him, he came too far into shore and was thrown by the waves high and dry on the sand. The Dolphin, eager in pursuit, and unable to stop himself, was also stranded. The Flying-Fish, beholding the Dolphin in the same condition as himself, said, "Now I die with pleasure, for I see my enemy has met the same fate."

Revenge is sweet.

THE ONE-EYED DOE

A Doe that had but one eye used to graze near the sea, so that she might keep her blind eye towards the water, while with the good eye she surveyed the country and saw that no hunters came near. It happened, however, that some men in a boat saw her, and as she did not perceive their approach, they came close enough to wound her. In her dying agony she cried out, "Alas, hard fate! That I should receive

The Miser

my death-wound from the side whence I expected no ill, and be safe on that where I looked for most danger."

Guard well the strong places.

THE FOX AND THE WOODCUTTER

A Fox having been hunted hard and run a long chase saw a Woodcutter at work, and begged him to help him to some hiding-place. The Man said he might go into his cottage, which was close by. He was no sooner in, than the Huntsmen came up. "Have you seen a Fox pass this way?" said they. The Woodcutter said "No," but pointed at the same time towards the place where the Fox lay. The Huntsmen did not take the hint, however, and made off again at full speed. The Fox, who had seen all that took place through a chink in the wall, thereupon came out, and was walking away without a word. "Why, how now?" said the Man; "haven't you the manners to thank your host before you go?" "Yes, yes," said the Fox; "if your deeds had been as honest as your words, I would have given you thanks."

Sincerity is shown by the heart.

THE POWER OF FABLES

Demades, a famous Greek orator, was once addressing an assembly at Athens on a subject of great importance, and in vain tried to fix the attention of his hearers. They laughed among themselves, watched the sports of the children, and in twenty other ways showed their want of concern in the subject of the discourse. Demades, after a short pause, spoke as follows: "Ceres one day journeyed in company with a Swallow and an Eel." At this there was marked attention, and every ear strained now to catch the words of the orator. "The party came to a river," continued he. "The Eel swam across, and the Swallow flew over." He then resumed the subject of his harangue. A great cry,

The Fox and the Woodcutter

however, arose from the people. "And Ceres? And Ceres?" cried they. "What did Ceres do?" "Why, the goddess was, and indeed she is now," replied he, "mightily offended that people should have their ears open to any sort of foolery, and shut to words of truth and wisdom."

Learn to listen wisely.

THE ASS, THE DOG, AND THE WOLF

A laden Ass was jogging along, followed by his tired master, at whose heels came a hungry Dog. Their path lay across a meadow, and the Man stretched himself out on the turf and went to sleep. The Ass fed on the pasture, and was in no hurry at all to move. The Dog alone, being gnawed by the pangs of hunger, found the time pass heavily. "Pray, dear companion," said he to the Ass, "stoop down, that I may take my dinner from the pannier." The Ass turned a deaf ear, and went on cropping away the green and tender grass. The Dog persisted, and at last the Ass replied, "Wait, can't you, till our master wakes. He will give you your usual portion, without fail." Just then a famished Wolf appeared upon the scene, and sprang at the throat of the Ass. "Help, help, dear Towzer!" cried the Ass; but the Dog would not budge. "Wait till our master wakes," said he; "he will come to your help, without fail." The words were no sooner spoken, than the Ass lay strangled upon the sod.

Favors beget favors.

AESOP AT PLAY

An Athenian once found Aesop joining merrily in the sports of some children. He ridiculed him for his want of gravity, and Aesop good-temperedly took up a bow, unstrung it, and laid it at his feet. "There, friend," said he; "that bow, if kept always strained, would lose its spring, and probably snap. Let it go free sometimes, and it will be the fitter for use when it is wanted."

Wise play makes wise work.

THE FOX AND THE APE

Upon the decease of the Lion, the Beasts of the Forest assembled to choose another king. The Ape made so many grimaces, and played so many antic tricks, that he was elected by a large majority, and the crown was placed upon his head. The Fox, envious of this distinction, seeing soon after a trap baited with a piece of meat, approached the new king, and said with mock humility, "May it please your majesty, I have found on your domain a treasure to which, if you will deign to accompany me, I will conduct you." The Ape thereupon set off with the Fox, and on arriving at the spot, laid his paw upon the meat. Snap! Went the trap, and caught him by the fingers. Mad with the shame and the pain, he called the Fox a thief and a traitor. The Fox laughed heartily and, going off, said over his shoulder, with a sneer, "You a king, and not understand a trap!"

Those who cannot manage their own affairs are unfit to manage others'.

THE GOATHERD AND THE GOATS

During a snowstorm in the depth of winter, a Goatherd drove his Goats for shelter to a large cavern in a rock. It happened that some wild Goats had already taken refuge there. The Man was so struck by the size and look of these Goats, and with their superior beauty to his own, that he gave to them all the food he could collect. The storm lasted many days, and the tame Goats, being entirely without food, died of starvation. As soon as the sun shone again, the strangers ran off, and made the best of their way to their native wilds. "Ungrateful beasts!" cried he, "is this the way you reward him who has served you?"

"How do we know," replied the last of the departing flock, "that you will not forsake your new friends in time of need, even as you forsook your old ones?" So the Goatherd had to go goatless home, and was well laughed at by all for his folly.

Be true to your own.

THE FOX AND THE TIGER

A skillful Archer, coming into the woods, directed his arrows so well that the beasts fled in dismay. The Tiger, however, told them not to be afraid, for he would singly engage their enemy, and drive him from their domain. He had scarcely spoken, when an arrow pierced his ribs and lodged in his side. The Fox asked him, slyly, what he thought of his opponent now. "Ah!" replied the Tiger, writhing with pain, "I find that I was mistaken in my reckoning."

Knowledge is power.

THE THIEF AND THE BOY

A Boy sat weeping upon the side of a well. A Thief happening to come by just at the same time, asked him why he wept. The Boy, sighing and sobbing, showed a bit of cord, and said that a silver tankard had come off from it, and was now at the bottom of the well. The Thief pulled off his clothes and went down into the well, meaning to keep the tankard for himself. Having groped about for some time without finding it, he came up again and found not only the Boy gone, but his own clothes also, the dissembling rogue having made off with them.

It takes a thief to catch a thief.

THE CAT AND THE COCK

A Cat one day caught a Cock, and resolved to make a meal of him. He first asked him, however, what defense he had to make. "What reason can you give," said he, "for your screaming at night so? No honest body can sleep for you." "Nay," answered the Cock, "I only crow in the service of man, to tell him when it is time to begin work." "What nonsense you talk!" said the Cat; "you are mistaken if you think that such an excuse as that will do me out of my breakfast."

No plea will protect the innocent from the unjust judge.

THE DOVE AND THE ANT

An Ant going to a river to drink, fell in, and was carried along in the stream. A Dove pitied her condition, and threw into the river a small twig, by means of which the Ant gained the shore. The Ant afterwards, seeing a man with a bow aiming at the Dove, stung him in the foot sharply, and made him miss his aim, and so saved the Dove's life.

The grateful heart will always find a way to be of service.

THE MICE IN COUNCIL

A certain Cat that lived in a large country-house was so vigilant and active that the Mice, finding their numbers grievously thinned, held a council, with closed doors, to consider what they had best do. Many plans had been started and dismissed, when a young Mouse, rising and catching the eye of the president, said that he had a proposal to make, that he was sure must meet with the approval of all. "If," said he, "the Cat wore around her neck a little bell, every step she took would make it tinkle; then, ever forewarned of her approach, we should have time to reach our holes. By this simple means we should live in safety, and defy her power." The speaker resumed his seat with a complacent air, and a murmur of applause arose from the audience. An old gray Mouse, with a merry twinkle in his eye, now got up, and said that the plan of the last speaker was an admirable one; but he feared it had one drawback. "My young friend has not told us," said he, "who is to put the bell on the Cat."

Counsel, to be wise, must be practical.

THE MOUNTAIN IN LABOR

In olden times a mighty rumbling was heard in a Mountain. This lasted a long time, until all the country round about was shaken. The people flocked together, from far and near, to see what would come of the upheaval. After many days of waiting and wise prophesyings from the crowd—out came a Mouse.

Do not make much ado about nothing.

THE CREAKING WHEEL

A Coachman hearing one of the Wheels of his coach make a great noise, and perceiving that it was the worst one of the four, asked how it came to take such a liberty. The Wheel answered that from the beginning of time grumbling had always been the privilege of the weak.

Much smoke, little fire.

A MAN BITTEN BY A DOG

A Man who had been sadly bitten by a Dog was advised by an old woman to cure the wound by rubbing a piece of bread in it, and giving it to the Dog that had bitten him. He did so, and Aesop, passing by at the time, asked him what he was about. The Man told him, and Aesop

The Mountain in Labor

replied, "I am glad you do it privately, for if the rest of the Dogs of the town were to see you, we should be eaten up alive."

Season counsel with sense.

THE FARMER AND HIS SONS

A certain Farmer, lying at the point of death, called his Sons around him, and gave into their charge his fields and vineyards, telling them that a treasure lay hidden somewhere in them, within a foot of the surface of the ground. His Sons thought he spoke of money that he had hidden, and after he was buried, they dug most industriously all over the estate, but found nothing. The soil being so well loosened, however, the succeeding crops were of unequalled richness, and the Sons then found out what their Father had in view in telling them to dig for hidden treasure.

Industry is Fortune's right hand.

THE PARTRIDGE AND THE GAMECOCKS

A certain man, having taken a Partridge, cut his wings and put him into a little yard where he kept Gamecocks. The Gamecocks were not at all civil to the newcomer, who at first put his treatment down to the fact of his being a stranger. When, however, he found that they frequently fought and nearly killed each other, he ceased to wonder that they did not respect him.

Those who do not treat their own kindred well make poor friends.

THE MOUSE AND THE WEASEL

A lean and hungry Mouse once pushed his way, not without some trouble, through a small hole into a corn-crib, and there fed for

some time so busily that, when he would have returned by the same
way he entered, he found himself too plump to get through the hole,
push as hard as he might. A Weasel, who had great fun in watching the
vain struggles of his fat friend, called to him, and said, "Listen to me,
my good Mouse. There is but one way to get out, and that is to wait till
you have become as lean as when you first got in."

The remedy is often as bad as the disease.

THE HUNTED BEAVER

The tail of the Beaver was once thought to be of use in medicine,
and the animal was often hunted on that account. A shrewd old
fellow of the race, being hard pressed by the Dogs, and knowing well
why they were after him, had the resolution and the presence of
mind to bite off his tail, and leave it behind him, and thus escaped
with his life.

The skin is dearer than the cloak.

THE FROGS DESIRING A KING

The Frogs, living an easy, free sort of life among the lakes and ponds,
once prayed Jupiter to send them a King. Jupiter, being at that time
in a merry mood, threw them a Log, saying as he did so, "There, then,
is a King for you." Awed by the splash, the Frogs watched their King
in fear and trembling, till at last, encouraged by his stillness, one
more daring than the rest jumped upon the shoulder of his monarch.
Soon, many others followed his example, and made merry on the
back of their unresisting King. Speedily tiring of such a torpid ruler,
they again petitioned Jupiter, and asked him to send them something more like a King. This time he sent them a Stork, who chased
them about and gobbled them up as fast as he could. They lost no

The Frogs Desiring a King

time, therefore, in beseeching the god to give them again their former state. "No, no," replied he; "a King that did you no harm did not please you. Make the best of the one you have, or you may chance to get a worse in his place."

Let well enough alone.

THE OLD MAN AND HIS SONS

An Old Man had several Sons, who were always falling out with one another. He had often, but to no purpose, exhorted them to live together in harmony. One day he called them round him, and producing a bundle of sticks, bade them try each in turn to break it across. Each put forth all his strength, but the bundle resisted their efforts. Then, cutting the cord which bound the sticks together, he told his Sons to break them separately. This was done with the greatest ease. "See, my Sons," exclaimed he, "the power of unity! Bound together by brotherly love, you may defy almost every mortal ill; divided, you will fall a prey to your enemies."

A house divided against itself cannot stand.

THE BEAR AND THE BEEHIVES

A Bear that had found his way into a garden where Bees were kept began to turn over the Beehives and devour the honey. He paid no attention to the first Bees which came to attack him; or to the threats from others. But finally the Bees settled in swarms about his head, and stung his eyes and nose so much, that, maddened with pain, he tore the skin from his head with his own claws.

Despise not little things.

The Bear and the Beehives

THE GEESE AND THE CRANES

A flock of Geese and a covey of Cranes used to feed together in a wheat field, where the grain was just ripening for harvest. One day the owner of the field came up and surprised them. The Cranes were thin and light, and easily flew away. But the Geese were heavy and fat, and many of them were caught.

Many criminals go unpunished.

THE TWO RABBITS

A Rabbit who was about to have a family entreated another Rabbit to lend her her hutch until she was able to move about again, and assured her that she should then have it without fail. The other very readily consented, and, with a great deal of civility, resigned it to her immediately. When the time was up, she came and paid the first Rabbit a visit, and very modestly intimated that now she was up and well she hoped she might have her hutch again, for it was really inconvenient for her to be without it any longer; she must therefore be so free as to desire her to provide herself with other lodgings as soon as she could. The other replied that she truly was ashamed of having kept her so long out of her own house, but it was not upon her own account (for, indeed, she was well enough to go anywhere) so much as that of her young, who were yet so weak that she was afraid they would not be able to follow her; and if she would be so good as to let her stay a fortnight longer she should take it for the greatest obligation in the world. The second Rabbit was so good-natured and compassionate as to comply with this request too, but at the end of the term, came and told her positively that she must turn out, for she could not possibly let her be there a day longer. "Must turn out!" says the other; "we will see about that, for I promise you, unless you can beat me and my whole litter of young, you are never likely to have anything more to do here."

Majorities promote tyranny.

THE OLD WOMAN AND HER MAIDS

A certain Old Woman had several Maids, whom she used to call to their work every morning at the crowing of the Cock. The Maids, finding it grievous to have their sweet sleep disturbed so early, killed the Cock, thinking when he was quiet they should enjoy their warm beds a little longer. But the Old Woman, no longer knowing what time it was, woke them up thereafter in the middle of the night.

Beware of falling from bad to worse.

THE HORSE AND THE ASS

A warhorse, gaily caparisoned, with arching neck and lofty tread, the ground ringing beneath his hoofs, overtook a patient Ass, slowly walking along under a heavy load. "Out of my way!" cried the Horse in a haughty tone, "and give me room to pass." The poor Ass did as he was told, sighing at the inequality of their lots. Not long after, he met the same Horse near the same spot; but in how different circumstances! Wounded in battle, and his master killed, he was now lame, half blind, heavily laden, and driven with many blows by a brutal carrier, into whose hands he had fallen.

Pride goes before a fall.

HERCULES AND THE WAGONER

As a Wagoner was driving his team through a miry lane, the wheels stuck fast in the clay, and the Horses could get on no further. The Man dropped on his knees, and began crying and praying to Hercules with all his might to come and help him. "Lazy fellow!" said Hercules, "get up and stir yourself. Whip your Horses stoutly, and put your shoulder to the wheel. If you want my help then, you shall have it."

Heaven helps those who help themselves.

THE BOAR AND THE ASS

A little scamp of an Ass, meeting in a forest with a Boar, came up to him and hailed him with impudent familiarity. The Boar was about to resent the insult by ripping up the Ass' flank, but, wisely keeping his temper, he contented himself with saying, "Go, you sorry beast; I could easily teach you manners, but I do not care to foul my tusks with the blood of so base a creature."

Scoffs are best paid with disdain.

THE ENVIOUS AND THE COVETOUS

Two Men, one a covetous fellow and the other thoroughly possessed by the passion of envy, came together to present their petitions to Jupiter. The god sent Apollo to deal with their requests. Apollo told them that whatsoever should be granted to the first who asked, the other should receive double. The Covetous Man forbore to speak, waiting in order that he might receive twice as much as his companion. The Envious Man, in the spitefulness of his heart, thereupon prayed that one of his own eyes might be put out, knowing that the other would have to lose both of his.

Envy shoots at another and wounds itself.

THE PORCUPINE AND THE SNAKES

A Porcupine, seeking shelter, desired some Snakes to give him admittance into their cave. They accordingly let him in, but were afterwards so annoyed by his sharp, prickly quills, that they repented of their hospitality, and asked him to withdraw and leave them their hole to themselves. "No," said he, "you may quit the place if you don't like it; for my part, I am very well satisfied where I am."

Be cautious in your choice of friends.

THE EAGLE AND THE FOX

An Eagle, looking around for something to feed her young ones with, spied a Fox's cub basking in the sun. She swooped upon him, and was about to carry him off, when the old Fox came up, and, with tears in her eyes, implored the Eagle, by the love which she, as a mother, felt for her own young, to spare this, her only child. The Eagle, whose nest was in a very high tree, made light of the Fox's prayers, and carried the cub to her brood. She was about to divide it among them, when the Fox, bent upon revenge, ran to an altar in a neighboring field on which some country people had been sacrificing a kid, and seizing thence a flaming brand, made towards the tree, meaning to set it on fire. The Eagle, terrified at the approaching ruin of her family, was glad to give back the cub, safe and sound, to his mother.

Measure for measure.

THE PEACOCK AND THE CRANE

The Peacock, spreading his gorgeous tail, stalked up and down in his most stately manner before a Crane, and ridiculed him for the plainness of his plumage. "I am robed like a king," said he, "in gold and purple and all the colors of the rainbow, while, just look at your plain coat!" "Tut, tut!" said the Crane; "which is the better now, to strut about in the dirt, and be gazed at by children, or to soar above the clouds, as I do?"

Appearances are deceitful.

THE MULE

A Mule, well fed and worked but little, frisked and gambolled about in the fields, and said to himself, "What strength, what spirits are mine! My father must surely have been a thoroughbred Horse." He soon after fell into the hands of another master, and was worked hard and but scantily fed. Thoroughly jaded, he now said, "What could I have been thinking about the other day? I feel certain now that my father could only have been an Ass."

Depend not on ancestry.

MERCURY AND THE WOODMAN

A Man felling a tree on the bank of a river by chance let his axe slip from his hand. It dropped into the water, and sank to the bottom. In great distress at the loss of his tool, he sat down on the bank and grieved bitterly, when Mercury appeared and asked him what was the matter. Having heard the Man's story, he dived to the bottom of the river, and bringing up a golden axe, offered it to him. "That is not mine," said the Woodman, and he refused to take it. Mercury dived a second time, and brought up a silver one. "That is not mine either," said the Man. Mercury dived a third time, and brought up the axe that the Man had lost, and this one he took with great joy and thankfulness. "Thou hast been so truthful," said Mercury, pleased with his honesty, "that I shall give thee not only thine own axe but also those of gold and silver." The Woodman told this adventure to his mates, and one of them at once set off for the river, and let his axe fall in on purpose. He then began to lament his loss with a loud voice. Mercury appeared, as before, and demanded the cause of his grief. After hearing the Man's account, he dived and brought up a golden axe, and asked him if that were his. "Yes! Yes!" said the covetous fellow, and greedily attempted to snatch it. "Dost thou think to deceive one who sees thy heart? "said Mercury sternly, and he not only declined to give the golden axe to him, but refused to let him have his own again.

Dishonesty overreaches itself.

THE FALCONER AND THE PARTRIDGE

A Partridge, being taken in the net of a Falconer, begged hard of the Man to be set free, and promised if he were let go to decoy other Partridges into the net. "No," replied the Falconer; "I did not mean to spare you; but, if I had, your words would now have condemned you. The scoundrel who, to save himself, offers to betray his friends, deserves worse than death."

Better a death with honor than a life with shame.

THE BOY WHO CRIED WOLF

A mischievous Lad, who was set to mind some Sheep, used to cry in jest, "The Wolf! The Wolf!" When the people came running to the spot, he would laugh at them for their pains. One day the Wolf came in reality, and the Boy this time called "The Wolf! The Wolf!" in earnest; but the men, having been so often deceived, disregarded his cries, and the Sheep were left at the mercy of the Wolf.

A liar cannot be believed even when he speaks the truth.

JUPITER AND THE ASS

A certain Ass that belonged to a gardener was weary of carrying heavy burdens, and prayed to Jupiter to give him a new master. Jupiter granted his prayer, and gave him for master a tile-maker, who made him carry heavier burdens than before. Again he came to Jupiter, and besought him to grant him a milder master, or at any rate a different one. The god, laughing at his folly, thereupon made him over to a tanner. The Ass was worked harder than ever, and soon upbraided himself for his stupidity. "Now," said he, "I have a master who not only beats me living, but who will not spare my hide even when I am dead."

Nothing is so bad that it might not be worse.

Mercury and the Woodman

THE HAWK AND THE FARMER

A Hawk, pursuing a Pigeon with great eagerness, was caught in a net which had been set in a cornfield for the Crows. The Farmer, seeing the Hawk fluttering in the net, came and took him. The Hawk besought the Man to let him go, saying piteously that he had done him no harm. "And pray what harm had the poor Pigeon you followed done to you?" replied the Farmer. Without more ado he wrung off his head.

Do unto others as you would have them do to you.

THE LARK AND HER YOUNG ONES

A Lark, who had Young Ones in a field of wheat that was almost ripe, was afraid lest the reapers should come before her young brood was fledged. Every day, therefore, when she flew away to look for food, she charged them to take notice of what they heard in her absence, and to tell her of it when she returned. One day when she was gone, they heard the master of the field say to his son that the grain seemed ripe enough to be cut, and tell him to go early tomorrow and desire their friends and neighbors to come and help to reap it. When the old Lark came home, the Little Ones fell quivering and chirping around her, and told her what had happened, begging her to remove them as fast as she could. The mother bade them to be easy, "for," said she, "if he depends upon his friends and his neighbors, I am sure the wheat will not be reaped tomorrow." Next day she went out again, and left the same orders as before. The owner came, and waited. The sun grew hot, but nothing was done, for not a soul came. "You see," said he to his son, "these friends of ours are not to be depended upon, so run off at once to your uncles and cousins, and say I wish them to come betimes tomorrow morning and help us to reap." This the Young Ones, in a great fright, reported also to their mother. "Do not be frightened, children," said she; "kindred and relations are not always very forward in helping one another; but keep your ears open, and let me know what you hear tomorrow." The owner came the next day, and, finding his relations as backward as his neighbors, said to his son,

"Now, George, listen to me. Get a couple of good scythes ready against tomorrow morning, for it seems we must reap the wheat ourselves." The Young Ones told this to their mother. "Then, my dears," said she, "it is indeed time for us to go, for when a man undertakes to do his business himself, it is not so likely that he will be disappointed." She at once removed her Young Ones, and the wheat was reaped the next day by the old man and his son.

He who would have things well done must do them himself.

THE LION AND THE FROG

The Lion hearing an odd kind of a hollow voice, and seeing nobody, started up. He listened again; the voice continued, and he shook with fear. At last seeing a Frog crawl out of the lake, and finding that the noise proceeded from that little creature, he crushed it to pieces with his feet.

Imaginary terrors fill a timorous soul with real fear.

THE SERPENT AND THE MAN

The Child of a villager, while at play in a field at the back of his Father's house, by chance trod upon a Snake, which turned round and bit him. The Child died of the bite, and the Father, pursuing the Snake, aimed a blow at him, and cut off a piece of his tail. The Snake gained his hole, and the next day the Man came and laid at the mouth of the hole some honey, meal, and salt, and made offers of peace, thinking to entice the Snake forth and kill him. "It won't do," hissed out the Snake. "As long as I miss my tail, and you your Child, there can be no goodwill between us."

A false truce is worse than battle.

The Lion and the Frog

THE ARCHER AND THE DOVE

An Archer, seeing a Dove among the branches of an oak, raised his bow and aimed at the Bird. Just then an Adder, on which unknowingly he had trodden, bit him in the leg. Feeling the poison spreading in his veins, he threw down his bow, and exclaimed, "Fate has justly brought destruction on me while I was contriving the death of another!"

He that mischief hatcheth, mischief always catcheth.

THE ASS EATING THISTLES

An Ass laden with very choice provisions, which he was carrying in harvest-time to the field for his master and the reapers, stopped by the way to eat a large and strong Thistle that grew by the roadside. "Many people would wonder," said he, "that with such delicate viands within reach, I do not touch them; but to me this bitter and prickly Thistle is more savory and relishing than anything else in the world."

What is one man's poison is another man's meat.

THE THRUSH AND THE SWALLOW

A young Thrush who lived in an orchard once became acquainted with a Swallow. A friendship sprang up between them, and the Swallow, after skimming the orchard and the neighboring meadow, would every now and then come to visit the Thrush. The Thrush, hopping from branch to branch, would welcome him with his most cheerful note. "Oh, mother!" said he to his parent, one day, "never did any creature have such a friend as I have in this same Swallow." "Nor did any mother," replied the parent Bird, "ever have such a silly son as I have in this same Thrush. Long before the approach of winter, your friend will have left you, and while you sit shivering on a leafless bough, he will be sporting under sunny skies hundreds of miles away."

Unequal friendships do not last.

THE CITY MOUSE AND THE COUNTRY MOUSE

A Country Mouse—a plain, sensible sort of fellow—was once visited by a former friend of his, who lived in a neighboring city. The Country Mouse put before his friend some fine peas and wheat-stalks, and called upon him to eat heartily of the good cheer. The City Mouse nibbled a little here and there in a dainty manner, wondering at the pleasure his host took in such coarse and ordinary fare. Finally the City Mouse said to his host, in their after-dinner chat, "Really, my good friend, I am surprised that you can keep in such spirits in this dismal, dead-and-alive kind of place. You see here no life, no gayety, no society in short, but go on and on, in a dull, humdrum sort of way, from one year's end to another. Come now with me this very night, and see with your own eyes what a life I lead." The Country Mouse consented, and as soon as it was dark, off they started for the city, where they arrived just at the end of a splendid supper given by the master of the house where our town friend lived. The City Mouse soon got together a heap of dainties on a corner of the handsome carpet. The Country Mouse, who had never even heard the names of half the meats set before him, was hesitating where he should begin, when the room door creaked, opened, and in entered a servant with a light. Off ran the Mice; but everything soon being quiet again, they returned to their repast, when once more the door opened, and the son of the master of the house came running in, followed by his little Terrier, who ran sniffing to the very spot where our friends had just been. The City Mouse was by that time safe in his hole—which, by the way, he had not been thoughtful enough to show to his friend, who could find no better shelter than that afforded by a sofa, behind which he waited in fear and trembling till quiet was again restored. The City Mouse then called upon him to resume his supper, but the Country Mouse said, "No, no; I shall be off as fast as I can. I would rather have my wheat-stalk with peace and security, than all your fine things in the midst of such alarms and frights as these."

A crust with quietness is better than a feast eaten in fear.

THE SWALLOW AND THE OTHER BIRDS

A Farmer sowing his fields with flax was observed by a Swallow, who, like the rest of her tribe, had traveled a good deal and was very clever. Among other things, she knew that of this same flax, when it grew up, nets and snares would be made, to entrap her little friends, the Birds of the country. Hence, she earnestly besought them to help her in picking up and eating the hateful seed, before it had time to spring from the ground. But food of a much nicer kind was then so plentiful, and it was so pleasant to fly about and sing, thinking of nothing, that they paid no attention to her entreaties. By and by the blades of the flax appeared above the ground, and the anxiety of the Swallow was renewed. "It is not yet too late," said she; "pull it all up, blade by blade, and you may then escape the fate which is otherwise in store for you. You cannot, like me, fly to other countries when danger threatens you here." The little Birds, however, took no notice of the Swallow, except to consider her a very troublesome person, whom silly fears had set beside herself. In the course of time the flax grew, ripened, and was gathered, spun, and made up into nets, as the Swallow had foretold. When the nets were set, the Birds could scarcely venture forth without some of their number being caught; and many a little captive thought, in dying, of the Swallow they held to be so crazy. While the Swallow, in despair at their thoughtless ways, has since preferred the society of men to that of her former companions.

Prevention is better than cure.

THE WOLVES AND THE SHEEP

Once upon a time, the Wolves sent an embassy to the Sheep, desiring that there might be a lasting peace between them. "Why," said the Messengers, "should we be forever at war? These wicked Dogs are the cause of it all; they are always barking at us and making us mad. Now if you will give up your Dogs, we will send you our children as hostages of peace." The silly Sheep agreed to the proposal and dismissed the Dogs. The Wolves gave up their Whelps. But the young Wolves cried for their mothers, and the Wolves then claimed that the peace had been broken, and set upon the Sheep, who, deprived of their defenders, the Dogs, could make no resistance, but fell an easy prey to their enemies.

Make no truce with a sworn enemy.

THE SOW AND THE WOLF

A Sow lay one day in the sty with her whole litter of pigs about her. A Wolf who longed for a small porker, but knew not how to get it, tried to worm himself into the good opinion of the mother. "How do you find yourself today, Mrs. Sow?" said he. "A little fresh air would certainly do you great good. Now, do go abroad and air yourself a little, and I will gladly mind your children till you return." "Many thanks for your offer," replied the Sow. "I know very well what kind of care you would take of my little ones, but if you really wish to be as obliging as you pretend to be, you will not show me your face again."

Services from strangers are to be suspected.

THE YOUNG MAN AND HIS CAT

A Young Man became so fond of his Cat that he made her his constant companion, and used to declare that if she were a woman he would marry her. Venus at length, seeing how sincere was his affection, gratified his wishes, and changed the Cat into a young and beautiful woman. The Young Man was delighted, and lost no time in marrying her. They lived happily together until one day when the Bride heard a Mouse in the room. Quickly springing up, she caught the Mouse, and killed it. Venus, angry at this behavior, and seeing that under the form of a woman there was still hidden the nature of a Cat, determined that form and nature should no longer disagree, and changed her back again to a Cat.

The true nature, though hidden, will assert itself.

THE FOX AND THE GRAPES

A hungry Fox one day chanced to come into a vineyard where he saw some fine ripe grapes hanging at a good height from the ground. He jumped at them, and made many other vain attempts to reach them. Finally he walked off grumbling to himself, "If those grapes had been good I would be disappointed. But they are green and sour."

It is easy to despise what you cannot get.

THE MAN AND THE FOX

A Man whose vines and orchards had suffered greatly from the ravages of Foxes one day caught one of these animals in a trap. In a great rage he tied up the Fox's tail with tow that had been steeped in turpentine, set a light to it, and let him run. Mad with pain and fright, the Fox ran through a large field in which, ripe for the harvest, stood corn belonging to his tormentor. The corn caught fire, and the flames, fanned by the wind, spread over the field and laid it waste. The Man lamented bitterly that he had not chosen some safer and less cruel means of revenge.

Do not let your anger crush your wisdom.

THE SENSIBLE ASS

An Old Fellow, in time of war, was allowing his Ass to feed in a green meadow, when he was alarmed by a sudden advance of the enemy. He

The Fox and the Grapes

tried every means in his power to urge the Ass to fly, but in vain. "The enemy are upon us," said he. "And what will the enemy do?" asked the Ass. "Will they put two pairs of panniers on my back, instead of one?" "No," answered the Man, "there is no fear of that." "Why then," replied the Ass, "I'll not stir an inch. I am born to be a slave, and my greatest enemy is he who gives me most to carry."

Conquest has no terror for slaves.

THE DOG AND THE SHEEP

The Dog sued the Sheep for a debt. The Kite and the Wolf were the judges, and the Fox and the Vulture were witnesses. Without going into the merits of the case, judgment was speedily given to the Dog, and debt, costs, and expenses of witnesses were all paid out of the body of the poor Sheep.

Evil men will side with one another against the powerful innocent.

THE PEACOCK AND THE MAGPIE

The Birds once met together to choose a king, and among others the Peacock was a candidate. Spreading his showy tail, and stalking up and down with affected grandeur, he caught the eyes of the silly multitude by his brilliant appearance, and was elected by acclamation. Just as they were going to proclaim him, the Magpie stepped forth into the midst of the assembly, and thus addressed the new king: "May it please your majesty-elect to permit a humble admirer to propose a question. As our king, we put our lives and fortunes in your hands. If, therefore, the Eagle, the Vulture, and the Kite should in the future, as they have in times past, make a descent upon us, what means would you take for our defense?" This pithy question opened the eyes of the Birds to the weakness of their choice. They cancelled the election, and have ever since regarded the Peacock as a vain pretender, and considered the Magpie to be as good a speaker as any of their number.

The crowd is caught by display.

THE ASS LADEN WITH SALT AND SPONGES

A Man drove his Ass to the seaside, and having purchased there a load of Salt, proceeded on his way home. In crossing a stream the Ass stumbled and fell. It was some time before he regained his feet, and by that time the Salt had all melted away, and he was delighted to find that he had lost his burden. A little while after that, the Ass, when laden with Sponges, had occasion to cross the same stream. Remembering his former good luck, he stumbled this time on purpose, and was surprised to find that his load, so far from disappearing, became many times heavier than before.

The same ploy does not often succeed twice.

THE EAGLE AND THE CROW

A Crow watched an Eagle swoop with a majestic air from a cliff upon a flock of Sheep, and carry away a Lamb in his talons. The whole thing looked so graceful and so easy that the Crow at once proceeded to imitate it, and pouncing upon the back of the largest and fattest Ram he could see, he tried to make off with it. He found that he could not move the Ram; and his claws got so entangled in the animal's fleece, that he could not get away himself. He therefore became an easy prey to the Shepherd, who, coming up at the time, caught him, cut his wings, and gave him to his children for a plaything. They came crowding about their Father and asked him what strange Bird that was. "Why," said he, "he'll tell you himself that he's an Eagle. But you take my word for it—I know him to be a Crow."

'Tis folly to attempt what you are unable to perform.

The Eagle and the Crow

THE LION, AND THE ASSES AND HARES

Upon the breaking out of a war between the Birds and the Beasts, the Lion summoned all his subjects to appear in arms at a certain time and place, upon pain of his high displeasure. A number of Hares and Asses made their appearance on the field. Several of the commanders were for turning them off as creatures utterly unfit for service. "Do not be too hasty," said the Lion; "the Asses will do very well for trumpeters, and the Hares will make excellent messengers."

Everything has its use.

THE GNAT AND THE BULL

A sturdy Bull was driven by the heat of the weather to wade up to his knees in a cool and swift-running stream. He had not long been there when a Gnat, that had been disporting itself in the air, pitched upon one of his horns. "My dear fellow," said the Gnat, with as great a buzz as he could manage, "pray excuse the liberty I take. If I am too heavy, only say so, and I will go at once and rest upon the poplar which grows hard by at the edge of the stream." "Stay or go, it makes no difference to me," replied the Bull. "Had it not been for your buzz, I should not even have known you were there."

Some men are more important in their own eyes
than in those of their neighbor's.

THE TRUMPETER TAKEN PRISONER

Upon the defeat of an army in battle, a Trumpeter was taken prisoner. The soldiers were about to put him to death, when he cried, "Nay, gentlemen, why should you kill me? This baud of mine is guiltless of a single life." "Yes," replied the soldiers; "but with that braying instrument of yours you incite others, and you must share the same fate as they."

Those who aid are as guilty as those who do evil.

THE FOWLER AND THE BLACKBIRD

A Fowler setting his nets in order was curiously watched by a Blackbird, who could not forbear coming and asking the Man civilly what he was about. "I am making a nice little house for such as you," answered the Fowler, "and putting into it food and all manner of useful things." He then departed and hid himself. The Blackbird, believing his words, came into the nets and was taken. "If your house is built for treachery," said he to the Man, "I hope it will have few inhabitants."

Dishonest rulers overthrow the state.

THE HORSE AND THE LADEN ASS

A full-fed lazy Horse was traveling along in company with a heavily laden Ass, belonging to the same master. The Ass, whose back was nearly breaking with his load, besought the Horse, for the sake of common kindness, to take a portion of it. The Horse, in his pride and ill nature, refused; and the poor Ass, after staggering on a little further, fell down and died. The master thereupon laid the whole of the burden upon the Horse's back, and the skin of the Ass besides.

Selfishness brings its own reward.

THE HARE AND THE TORTOISE

The Hare one day laughed at the Tortoise for his short feet, slowness and awkwardness. "Though you may be swift as the wind," replied the

Tortoise good-naturedly, "I can beat you in a race." The Hare looked on the challenge as a great joke, but consented to a trial of speed, and the Fox was selected to act as umpire, and hold the stakes. The rivals started, and the Hare, of course, soon left the Tortoise far behind. Having reached midway to the goal, she began to play about, nibble the young herbage, and amuse herself in many ways. The day being warm, she even thought she would take a little nap in a shady spot, for she thought that if the Tortoise should pass her while she slept, she could easily overtake him again before he reached the end. The Tortoise meanwhile plodded on, unwavering and unresting, straight towards the goal. The Hare, having overslept herself, started up from her nap, and was surprised to find that the Tortoise was nowhere in sight. Off she went at full speed, but on reaching the winning-post, found that the Tortoise was already there, waiting for her arrival.

Slow and steady wins the race.

THE SICK STAG

A Stag whose joints had become stiff with old age was at great pains to get together a large heap of fodder—enough, as he thought, to last him for the remainder of his days. He stretched himself out upon it and, now dozing, now nibbling, made up his mind to wait quietly for the end. He had always been of a gay and lively turn, and had made in his time many friends. These now came in great numbers to see him, and wish him farewell. While engaged in friendly talk over past adventures and old times, what more natural than that they should help themselves to a little of the food which seemed so plentifully stored around? The end of the matter was that the poor Stag died not so much of sickness or of old age as for sheer want of the food which his friends had eaten for him.

Thoughtless friends bring more hurt than profit.

THE PEACH, THE APPLE, AND THE BLACKBERRY

A dispute arose once between a Peach and an Apple as to which was the fairer fruit of the two. They were so loud in their wrangling that a Blackberry from the next hedge overheard them. "Come," said the Blackberry, who thought herself quite fine, also, "we are all friends, and all fair. Pray let us have no quarrels among ourselves."

Know thyself.

THE COCK AND THE FOX

One bright spring morning a Cock, perched among the branches of a lofty tree, crowed loud and long. The shrillness of his voice echoed through the wood, and the well-known note brought a Fox, who was prowling in quest of prey, to the spot. The Fox, seeing the Cock was at a great height, set his wits to work to find some way of bringing him down. He saluted the Bird in his mildest voice, and said, "Have you not heard, cousin, of the proclamation of peace and harmony among all kinds of Beasts and Birds? We are no longer to prey upon and devour one another, but love and friendship are to be the order of the day. Do come down, and we will talk over this great news at our leisure." The Cock, who knew that the Fox was only at his old tricks, pretended to be watching something in the distance. Finally the Fox asked him what it was he looked at so earnestly. "Why," said the Cock, "I think I see a pack of Hounds yonder." "Oh, then," said the Fox, "your humble servant; I must be gone." "Nay, cousin," said the Cock; "pray do not go: I am just coming down. You are surely not afraid of Dogs in these peaceable times!" "No, no," said the Fox; "but ten to one they have not heard of the proclamation yet."

'Tis a poor rule that will not work both ways.

The Cock and the Fox

MERCURY AND THE CARVER[4]

Mercury, having a mind to know how much he was esteemed among men, disguised himself, and going into a Carver's shop, where little images were sold, saw those of Jupiter, Juno, himself, and most of the other gods and goddesses. Pretending that he wanted to buy, he said to the Carver, pointing to the figure of Jupiter, "What do you ask for that?" "Ten pieces of silver," answered the Man. "And what for that?" meaning Juno. "Ah," said the Man, "I will let you have her for five pieces." "Well, and what is the price of this?" said Mercury, laying his hand on a figure of himself, with wings, rod, and all complete. "You ought to want more for him as he is a special patron of your craft." "Why," replied the Man, "if you really mean business, and will buy the other two, I'll throw you that fellow into the bargain."

A spy never learns good of himself.

THE FOX AND THE BOAR

A Boar stood whetting his tusks against an old Tree. The Fox, who happened to come by at the same time, asked him why he made those martial preparations of whetting his teeth, since there was no enemy near that he could perceive? "That may be, master Fox," said the Boar, "but we should scour up our arms while we have leisure, you know; for, in time of danger, we shall have something else to do."

The discreet man should have a reserve of everything that is necessary before the time comes for him to make use of them.

THE HEN AND THE SWALLOW

There was once a foolish Hen, that sat brooding upon a nest of Snakes' eggs. A Swallow, perceiving it, flew to her and told her what danger she was in. "Silly creature," said she, "you are hatching vipers.

The Fox and the Boar

The moment they see the light, they will turn and wreak their venomous spite upon you."

Beware the consequences of your actions.

THE BEES, THE DRONES, AND THE WASP

A party of Drones got into a hive, and laying claim to the honey and comb which they found there tried to force the Bees to quit. The Bees, however, made a sturdy resistance. Finally the Drones agreed to their proposal that the dispute should be referred for judgment to the Wasp. The Wasp, pretending that it was a hard matter to decide, directed both parties to make and fill some comb before him in court, so that he might see whose production most resembled the property in dispute. The Bees at once set to work, but the Drones refused the trial; so the verdict was given by Judge Wasp in favor of the Bees.

A tree is known by its fruit.

THE OLD MAN AND DEATH

A poor and toil-worn Peasant, bent with years, and groaning beneath the weight of a heavy faggot of firewood which he carried, sought, weary and sore-footed on a long and dusty road, to gain his distant cottage. Unable to bear the weight of his burden any longer, he let it fall by the roadside, and sitting down upon it, lamented his hard fate. What pleasure had he known since first he drew breath in this sad world? From dawn to dusk one round of ill-requited toil! At home, empty cupboards, a discontented wife, and disobedient children! He called on Death to free him from his troubles. At once the King of Terrors stood before him, and asked him what he wanted. Awed at the ghastly presence, the Old Man stammered out: "I—I—only wanted you to help me put this bundle of sticks on my shoulders again."

What is desired in fancy is often regretted in reality.

THE OLD WOMAN AND THE DOCTOR

An Old Woman who had bad eyes called in a clever Doctor who agreed for a certain sum to cure them. He was a very clever Doctor, but he was also a very great rogue; and when he called each day and bound up the Old Woman's eyes, he took advantage of her blindness to carry away with him some article of her furniture. This went on until he pronounced the Woman cured. Her room was then nearly bare. He claimed his reward, but the Old Lady protested that, so far from being cured, her sight was worse than ever. "We will soon see about that, my good Woman," said he; and she was shortly after summoned to appear in Court. "May it please your Honor," said she to the Judge, "before I called in this Doctor I could see a score of things in my room that now, when he says I am cured, I cannot see at all." This opened the eyes of the Court to the knavery of the Doctor, who was forced to give the Old Woman her property back again, and was not allowed to claim a penny of his fee.

Knavery overreaches itself.

THE WOLF IN SHEEP'S CLOTHING

A Wolf, wrapping himself in the skin of a Sheep, by that means got admission into a sheepfold, where he devoured several of the young Lambs. The Shepherd, however, soon found him out and hung him up to a tree, still in his disguise. Some other Shepherds passing that way thought it was a Sheep hanging, and cried to their friend, "What, brother! Is that the way you serve Sheep in this part of the country?" "No, friends," cried he, turning the hanging body around so that they might see what it was; "but it is the way to serve Wolves, even though they be dressed in Sheep's clothing."

The credit got by a lie lasts only till the truth comes out.

THE FROG AND THE MOUSE

A Frog and a Mouse, who had long been rivals for the sovereignty of a certain marsh, and had many a skirmish and running fight together, agreed one day to settle the matter, once for all, by a fair and open combat. They met, and each, armed with the point of a bulrush for a spear, was ready to fight to the death. The combat began in earnest, and there is no knowing how it might have ended, had not a Kite, seeing them from afar, pounced down and carried off both heroes in her talons.

Peace brings security.

THE ASS AND THE LION HUNTING

The Lion once took a fancy to go Hunting in company with an Ass. He sent the Ass into the forest, and told him to bray there as hard as he could. "By that means," said he, "you will rouse all the Beasts in the forest. I shall stand here, and catch all that fly this way." So the Ass brayed in his most hideous manner; and when the Lion was tired of slaughter, he called to him to come out of the wood. "Did I not do my part well?" asked the conceited Beast. "Excellently," replied the Lion. "Had I not known that you were nothing more than an Ass, I should have been frightened myself."

The braggart is not the fighter.

THE PRINCE AND THE PAINTED LION

A certain King had an only son, of whom he was dotingly fond. The Prince delighted in hunting, and went every day into the forest in chase of wild beasts. His father believed firmly in dreams, omens, and the like, and dreaming one night that his son was killed by a Lion, resolved that he should not go to the forest anymore. He therefore

The Ass and the Lion Hunting

built a spacious tower and kept the Prince there closely confined. That his captivity might be less tedious to bear, he surrounded him with books, music, and pictures; and on the walls of the tower were painted in lifesize all the beasts of the chase, and among the rest a Lion. The Prince stood one day gazing for a long time at this picture, and, in his rage at being imprisoned, he struck the painted Lion a violent blow with his fist, saying, "Thou, cruel beast, art the cause of all my grief! Had it not been for the lying dream of thee which came to my father, I should now be free." The point of a nail in the wainscot under the canvas entered his hand through the force of his blow; the wound became inflamed, and the youth died from its effects.

Fancied dangers lead to real ones.

THE ANGLER AND THE LITTLE FISH

A Fisherman who had caught a very small Fish was about to throw him into his basket. The little fellow, gasping, pleaded thus for his life: "What! You are never going to keep such a minnow as I am, not one quarter grown! Fifty like me wouldn't make a decent dish. Do throw me back, and come and catch me again when I am bigger." "It's all very well to say 'Catch me again,' my little fellow," replied the Man, "but you know you'll make yourself very scarce for the future. You're big enough now to make one in a frying-pan, so in you go."

No time like the present.

THE TWO TRAVELERS

As two Men were traveling through a wood, one of them took up an axe which he saw lying upon the ground. "Look here," said he to his companion, "I have found an axe." "Don't say 'I have found it,'" replied the other, "but 'We have found it.' As we are companions, we ought to share it between us." The first would not, however, consent. They had not gone far, when they heard the owner of the axe calling after them in a great passion. "We are in for it!" said he who had the axe. "Nay," answered the other, "say, 'I am in for it!' not 'we.' You would not let me share the prize, and I am not going to share the danger."

He who shares the danger ought to share the prize.

THE LION, THE FOX, AND THE WOLF

The King of the Forest was once long and seriously ill, and his majesty's temper not being at all improved by the trial, the Fox, with his usual discretion, kept away from Court as much as he could. He slunk about, however, as near as he was able without being seen, and one day overheard the Wolf talking to the Lion about him. The Wolf and the Fox were never good friends, and the Wolf was now calling the Lion's attention to the fact that the Fox had not shown his face for a long time at Court. "I have strong reasons for suspecting that he is busily engaged in hatching some treason or other," said the Wolf. The Lion thereupon commanded that the Fox should be brought at once to his presence; so the Jackal led him in. "What do you mean by not paying us court?" roared the Monarch. "Pardon, your majesty," replied the Fox, bowing low. "I did not absent myself from want of respect to you, but out of concern for your welfare. I have gone far and wide," he continued, "and consulted the finest doctors as to the best means of curing your malady." "Have you found a cure?" eagerly inquired the Lion. "They tell me," answered the Fox with a leer at the Wolf, "that the only way to save your majesty's life, is to wrap yourself in the warm skin of a newly slain Wolf." The Lion, eager to try the remedy, at once dragged the Wolf to him and killed him on the spot.

Evil is payable in evil.

THE THIEVES AND THE COCK

Some Thieves once broke into a house, and found nothing in it worth carrying off but a Cock. The poor Cock said as much for himself as a Cock could say, urging them to remember his services in calling people up to their work when it was time to rise. "Nay," said one of the Robbers, "you had better say nothing about that. You alarm people and keep them waking, so that it is impossible for us to rob in comfort."

The safeguards of virtue are hateful to the wicked.

THE FOX AND THE WOLF

A Wolf who lived in a cave, having laid in a good store of food, kept himself very close, and set to work to enjoy it. A Fox, who missed the Wolf from his usual haunts, at last found out where he was, and, under pretence of asking after his health, came to the mouth of the cave and peeped in. He expected to be asked inside to dinner, but the Wolf gruffly said that he was far too ill to see anybody. So the Fox trotted off again, in anything but a charitable state of mind. Away he went to a Shepherd, and told the Man to get a good stick and come with him, and he would show him where to find a Wolf. The Shepherd came accordingly, and killed the Wolf. The Fox took possession of the cave and its stores. But he did not long enjoy the fruits of his treachery, for the Man, passing by that way a few days after, looked into the cave, and seeing the Fox there, killed him too.

He who brings mischief invites mischief.

THE MAN AND HIS IDOL

A Poor Man who longed to be rich used to pray day and night for wealth to an Idol which he had in his house. Notwithstanding all his prayers, instead of becoming richer, he got poorer. Out of all patience with his Idol, he one day took it by the legs, and dashed it to pieces upon the floor, when hundreds of gold pieces, which had been hidden in the body, flew about the room. Overjoyed at the sight, he exclaimed, "How have I wasted my time in worshipping a god, who yields to force what he would not grant to prayers!"

Ask favors only of those who can grant them.

THE GNAT AND THE LION

"I am not afraid of you," once said the Gnat to the Lion. "You may be stronger than I, but I can conquer you, and all your cruel claws and sharp teeth will avail you nothing against my sting. Let us fight it out here and now." Having sounded his buzzing challenge, he at once attacked the Lion, whom he so enraged by stinging the most sensitive parts of his nose, eyes, and ears, that the Beast roared in anguish, and, maddened with pain, tore himself cruelly with his claws. All the attempts of the Lion to crush the Gnat were in vain, and the Insect returned again and again to the charge. At last the poor Beast lay exhausted and bleeding upon the ground. The Gnat, hovering over the spot, and sounding a note of triumph, happened to come in the way of the web of a Spider which, slight as it was, was enough to stop him in his career. His efforts to escape only fixed him more firmly in the toils, and he who had vanquished the Lion became the prey of the Spider.

Victory is not always lasting.

THE ANTS AND THE GRASSHOPPER

A Grasshopper that had merrily sung all the summer was almost perishing with hunger in the winter. So she went to some Ants that lived near, and asked them to lend her a little of the food they had put by. "You shall certainly be paid before this time of year comes again," said she. "What did you do all the summer?" asked they. "Why, all day long, and all night long too, I sang, if you please," answered the Grasshopper. "Oh, you sang, did you?" said the Ants. "Now, then, you can dance."

Provide today for the future.

THE HARE AND THE HOUND

A Dog having given a long chase to a fine Hare that showed himself to be a splendid runner was at length forced, by want of breath, to give over the pursuit. The owner of the Dog thereupon taunted him upon his want of spirit in having allowed himself to be beaten by the Hare. "Ah, master," answered the Dog, "you may laugh if you like, but we had not the same stake at hazard. He was running for his life, while I was only running for my dinner."

Fear lends wings.

THE KNIGHT AND THE CHARGER

A certain Soldier, in time of war, took great pains to keep his Horse well fed and cared-for, and in first-rate condition. When the war was over, the Soldier's pay was reduced, and he allowed his Horse, that had carried him nobly through many a hot engagement, to be used for dragging huge logs of timber, and for hire in many other rough and disagreeable ways. Being thus hardly fed and badly treated, the animal's strength and spirit fell away. It was not long before the war was renewed, and the Soldier, taking his Horse again, tried, by good feeding and better treatment, to make him into a battle-steed once more. There was not time for this, however; and the Horse, as his weak legs gave way under him in a charge, said to his master, "It is too late now to repair your neglect. You have degraded me from a Horse into an Ass. It is not my fault that I cannot at once turn back from an Ass to a Horse."

It is easier to go from good to bad than from bad to good.

THE LION AND THE ELEPHANT

The Lion complained most sadly that a Beast with such claws, teeth, and strength as he possessed, should yet be moved to a state of abject terror at the crowing of a Cock. "Can life be worth having," said he, "when so vile a creature has the power to rob it of its charms?" Just then, a huge Elephant came along, flapping his ears quickly to and fro, with an air of great concern. "What troubles you so?" said the Lion to the Elephant. "Can any mortal thing have power to harm a Beast so large as you?" "Do you see this little buzzing Gnat?" replied the Elephant; "let him but sting the inner part of my ear, and I shall go mad with pain." The Lion thereupon took heart again, and determined not to let troubles, which he shared in common with all created things, blind him to what was pleasant in life.

Brooding over troubles increases them.

JUPITER AND THE HERDSMAN

A Herdsman missing a young Cow that belonged to the herd went up and down the forest to seek it. Not being able to find it, he prayed to Jupiter, and promised to sacrifice a Kid if he would help him to find the thief. He then went on a little farther, and suddenly came upon a Lion, grumbling over the carcass of the Cow, and feeding upon it. "Great Jupiter!" cried the Man, "I promised thee a Kid, if thou wouldst show me the thief. I now offer thee a full-grown Bull, if thou wilt mercifully deliver me safe from his clutches."

The fulfillment of our wishes might lead to ruin.

THE SPARROW AND THE HARE

A Hare, being seized by an Eagle, cried out in a piteous manner. A Sparrow sitting on a tree close by, so far from pitying the poor animal, made merry at his expense. "Why did you stay there to be taken?" said he. "Could not so swift a creature as you have easily escaped from an Eagle?" Just then a Hawk swooped down and carried off the Sparrow, who, when he felt the Hawk's talons in his sides, cried still more loudly than the Hare. The Hare, in the agonies of death, received comfort from the fact that the fate of the mocking Sparrow was no better than his own.

When calamity overtakes the hard-hearted they receive no sympathy.

THE APE AND THE DOLPHIN

A Ship, wrecked off the coast of Greece, had on board a large Ape, kept for the diversion of the sailors. The ship went down, and the Ape, with most of the crew, was left struggling in the water. Dolphins are said to have a great friendship for man; and one of these fishes, taking the Ape for a man, came under him, and, supporting him on his back, swam with him to the mouth of the harbor of Piraeus. "In what part of Greece do you live?" demanded the Dolphin. "I am an Athenian," said the Ape. "Oh, then, you know Piraeus, of course?" said the Dolphin. "Know Piraeus!" said the Ape, not wishing to appear ignorant to the Dolphin; "I should rather think I did. Why, my father and he are first cousins." Thereupon the Dolphin, finding that he was supporting an impostor, slipped from beneath his legs, and left him to his fate.

The liar should take care to be well informed.

THE WOLVES AND THE SICK ASS

An Ass being sick, the report of it was spread abroad in the country, and some did not hesitate to say that she would die before the night was over. Upon this, several Wolves came to the stable where she lay, and rapping at the door inquired how she did. A young Ass thrust

The Wolves and the Sick Ass

her head out the window, and told them that her mother was much better than they desired.

Words reveal wishes.

THE FOX IN THE WELL

An unlucky Fox having fallen into a Well was able, by dint of great efforts, to keep his head barely above water. While he was there struggling, and sticking his claws into the side of the Well, a Wolf came by and looked in. "What! My dear brother," said he, with affected concern, "can it really be you that I see down there? How cold you must feel! How long have you been in? How came you to fall in? I am so pained to see you. Do tell me all about it!" "The end of a rope would be of more use to me than all your pity," answered the Fox. "Just help me to set my foot once more on solid ground, and you shall have the whole story."

Saying well is good, but doing well is better.

THE ASS CARRYING AN IDOL

The master of an Ass was employed to take an Idol from the shop of the sculptor where it was made to the temple in which it was to be placed. For this purpose it was put on the back of the Ass, and carried through the principal streets of the city. Seeing that all the people, as he went along, bent themselves in lowly reverence, the animal fancied that it was to him they were bowing. In consequence he pricked up his ears, flourished his tail, and felt as proud as might be. Finally he became so vain that he stood stock-still, and refused to leave his circle of supposed worshippers. The driver seeing him thus stop laid the whip lustily over his body, and said: "O, you obstinate fool! It is not yet come to this, that men do homage to an Ass!"

They are not wise who take to themselves the credit due to others.

THE CATS AND THE MICE

In former times a fierce and lasting war raged between the Cats and Mice, in which, time after time, the latter had to fly. One day when the Mice in council were discussing the cause of their ill-luck, the general opinion seemed to be that it was the difficulty of knowing, in the heat of the conflict, who were their leaders that led to their defeat and utter rout. So it was decided that in future each captain should have his head decorated with some thin straws, so that all the Mice would then know to whom they were to look for orders. After the Mice had drilled and disciplined their numbers, they once more gave battle to the Cats; but again they met with no better success, being utterly routed. The greater part reached their holes in safety, but the captains were prevented by their strange head-gear from entering their retreats, and fell prey to their cruel pursuers.

Those who have the greatest honor have the gravest danger.

THE DOG INVITED TO SUPPER

A certain rich man invited a person of high rank to sup with him. Great preparations were made for the repast, and all the delicacies of the season provided. The Dog of the host, having long wished to entertain another Dog, a friend of his, thought this would be a capital time to ask him to come. As soon, therefore, as it fell dusk, the invited Dog came, and was shown by his friend into the kitchen. The sight of the food there filled him with astonishment, and he resolved that when the time came, he would eat enough to last him a week. He wagged his tail so hard, and licked his chops with so much vigor, that he attracted the notice of the head cook, who, seeing a strange Dog about, caught him up by the tail, and after giving him a swing in the air, sent him flying through the open window into the street. He limped away, and was soon surrounded by a lot of Curs to whom he had boasted of his invitation. They asked him eagerly how he had fared. "Oh, rarely," answered he. "I was treated so warmly, that I hardly know how I got out of the house."

Beware how you accept favors!

THE LION, THE FOX, AND THE ASS

An Ass and a Fox were rambling through a forest one day, when they were met by a Lion. The Fox was seized with great fear, and taking the first opportunity of getting the ear of the Lion, thought to obtain his own safety at the expense of that of his companion. "Sire," said he, "yonder Ass is young and plump, and if your majesty would care to make a dinner off him, I know how he might be caught without much trouble. There is a pitfall not far away, into which I can easily lead him." The Lion agreed, and seeing the Ass securely taken, he began his dinner by devouring the traitorous Fox, reserving the Ass to be eaten at his leisure.

Traitors receive no consideration even from those whom they serve.

THE HORSE AND THE LION

A Lion, who had got old and infirm, saw a fine plump Nag, and longed for a bit of him. Knowing that the animal would prove too fleet for him in the chase, he had recourse to artifice. He gave out to all the Beasts that, having spent many years in studying physic, he was now prepared to heal any malady or distemper with which they might be afflicted. He hoped by that means to get admittance among them, and so find a chance of satisfying his appetite. The Horse, who had doubts of the Lion's honesty, came up limping, pretending that he had run a thorn into one of his hind feet, which gave him great pain. The Lion asked that the foot might be shown to him, and pored over it with a mock earnest air. The Horse, slyly looking round, saw that he was preparing to spring, and vigorously sending out both his heels at once, gave the Lion such a kick in the face, that it laid him stunned and sprawling upon the ground. Then laughing at the success of his trick, he trotted merrily away.

Over-craftiness defeats itself.

THE KID AND THE WOLF

A Kid, safely perched upon a high rock, bestowed all manner of abuse upon a Wolf on the ground below. After he had called him all the evil names he could think of, the Wolf, looking up, replied, "Do not think, foolish youngster, that you annoy me. I regard the ill language as coming not from you, but from the place upon which you stand."

The best answer for silly pretenders is disdain.

THE TAIL OF THE SERPENT

The tail of a Serpent once rebelled against the Head, and said that it was a great shame that one end of any animal should always have its way, and drag the other after it, whether it was willing or no. It was in vain that the Head urged that the Tail had neither brains nor eyes, and that it was in no way made to lead. Wearied by the Tail's importunity, the Head one day let him have his will. The Serpent now went backwards for a long time, quite gaily, until he came to the edge of a high cliff, over which both Head and Tail went flying, and came with a heavy thump on the shore beneath. The Head was never again troubled by the Tail with a word about leading.

Let those lead who are best fitted to lead.

THE GARDENER AND HIS DOG

A Gardener's Dog, frisking about the brink of a well in the garden, happened to fall in. The Gardener very readily ran to his assistance; but as he was trying to help him out, the Cur bit him on the hand. The Man, annoyed at what he considered such ungrateful behavior towards one whose only aim was to save his life, came away and left the Dog to drown.

Kindness should merit kindness.

THE OLD HOUND

An Old Hound, who had hunted well in his time, once seized a Stag, but from feebleness and the loss of his teeth was forced to let him go. The Master coming up began to beat the Old Dog cruelly, but left off when the poor animal addressed him as follows: "Hold, dear Master! You know well that neither my courage nor my will was at fault, but only my strength and my teeth, and these I have lost in your service."

Forget not past services.

THE GOURD AND THE PINE

A Gourd was planted close beside a large, well-spread Pine. The season was kindly, and the Gourd shot itself up in a short time, climbing by the boughs and twining about them, till it topped and covered the tree itself. The leaves were large, and the flowers and fruit fair, insomuch that the Gourd, comparing itself with the Pine, had the assurance to value itself above it. "Why," said the Gourd, "you have been more years growing to this stature than I have been days." "Well," replied the Pine, "but after the many winters and summers that I have endured, the many blasting colds and parching heats, you see me the very

The Old Hound

same thing that I was so long ago. But when you once come to the proof, the first blight or frost shall bring down that pride of yours, and strip you of all your glory."

Time tests merit.

THE MOUSE AND THE FROG

A Mouse and a Frog had lived some time in intimacy together, and the Frog had often visited the Mouse's quarters and been welcome to a share of his store. So the Frog invited the Mouse to his house in return; but as this was across the stream, the Mouse, alleging that he could not swim, had hitherto declined to go. The Frog, however, one day pressed him so much, offering at the same time to conduct him safely across, that the Mouse consented. One of the forefeet of the Mouse was accordingly bound to one of the hind-legs of the Frog by a stout blade of grass, and the friends set off to cross the stream. When about halfway across, it treacherously entered the Frog's head to try to drown the Mouse. He thought that by this means he should have undivided possession of the latter's stock of provisions. So he started for the bottom of the stream; but the struggles and cries of the Mouse attracted the attention of a Kite who was sailing above in the air. He descended and caught up the Mouse. The Frog, being tied to the Mouse, shared the same fate, and was justly punished for his treachery.

Harm hatch, harm catch.

THE GOAT AND THE LION

The Lion, seeing a Goat skipping about in high glee upon a steep craggy rock, called to him to come down upon the green pasture where he would be able to feed in much greater comfort. The Goat,

The Goat and the Lion

who saw through the design of the Lion, replied, "Many thanks for your advice, dear Lion, but I wonder whether you are thinking more of my comfort, or how you would relish a nice morsel of Goat's flesh."

Those who use trickery should not be surprised when it does not work.

THE FALCON AND THE GOOSE

A Goose who had strong reasons for thinking that the time of his sacrifice was near at hand carefully avoided coming into close quarters with any of the farm servants or domestics of the estate on which he lived. A glimpse that he had once caught of the kitchen, with its blazing fire, and the cook, chopping off the heads of some of his companions, had been sufficient to keep him ever after in dread. Hence, one day when he was wanted for roasting, all the calling, clucking, and coaxing of the cook's assistants were in vain. "How deaf and dull you must be," said a Falcon who noticed this, "not to hear when you are called, or to see when you are wanted! You should take pattern by me. I never let my master call me twice." "Ah," answered the Goose, "if Falcons were called, like Geese, to be run upon a spit and set before the kitchen fire, they would be just as slow to come, and just as hard of hearing, as I am now."

The errand makes the difference.

THE WOLF AND THE SHEEP

A Wolf that had been sorely worried and left for dead by the Dogs lay not far from a running stream. Parched with thirst, the babble of the brook sounded most temptingly in his ears, and he felt that one cool, delicious draught might yet restore to him some hope of life. Just then a Sheep passed near. "Pray, sister, bring me some water from yon stream," said he. "Water is all I want; I do not ask for meat." "Yes," replied the Sheep, "but I know very well that when I have brought you water, my body will serve for meat."

Hypocritical speeches are easily seen through.

THE SHEEP AND THE DOG

The Sheep one day complained to the Shepherd that while they were shorn of their fleece, and their young ones often taken and killed for food, they received nothing in return but the green herbage of the earth, which grew of itself, and cost him no pains to procure. "On the other hand, your Dog," said they, "which gives no wool, and is of no use for food, is petted and fed with as good meat as his master." "Peace, bleating simpletons!" replied the Dog, who overheard them; "were it not that I look after and watch you, and keep off Wolves and thieves, small good would be to you your herbage or anything else."

Each has his allotted labor.

THE TONGUES

Xanthus invited a large company to dinner, and Aesop was ordered to furnish the feast with the choicest dainties that money could procure. The first course consisted of Tongues, cooked in different ways, and served with appropriate sauces. This gave rise to a deal of mirth and witty remarks among the assembled guests. The second course, however, like the first, was also nothing but Tongues, and so the third, and the fourth. The matter seemed to all to have gone beyond a jest, and Xanthus angrily demanded of Aesop, "Did I not tell you, sirrah, to provide the choicest dainties that money could procure?" "And what excels the Tongue?" replied Aesop. "It is the great channel of learning and philosophy. By this noble organ, addresses and eulogies are made, and commerce, contracts, and marriages completely established. Nothing is equal to the Tongue." The company applauded Aesop's wit, and good-humor was restored. "Well," said Xanthus to the guests, "pray do me the favor of dining with me again tomorrow. And if this is your best," continued he, turning to Aesop, "pray, tomorrow let us have some of the worst meat you can find." The next day, when dinner-time came, the guests were assembled. Great was their astonishment, and great the anger of Xanthus, at finding that again nothing but Tongues was put upon the table. "How, sir," said Xanthus, "should Tongues be the best of meat one day and the worst another?" "What," replied Aesop, "can be worse than the Tongue? What wickedness is there under the sun that it has not a part in? Treasons, violence, injustice, and fraud are debated, resolved upon, and communicated by the Tongue. It is the ruin of empires, cities, and of private friendships." The company were more than ever struck by Aesop's ingenuity, and successfully interceded for him with his master.

A wise answer saves all.

AESOP AND HIS FELLOW SERVANTS

A Merchant who was at one time Aesop's master ordered all things to be got ready for an intended journey. When the burdens were being shared among the Servants, Aesop requested that he might have the lightest. He was told to choose for himself, and he took up the basket of bread. The other Servants laughed, for that was the largest and heaviest of all. When dinner-time came, Aesop, who had with some difficulty sustained his load, was told to distribute an equal share of bread all round. He did so, and this lightened his burden one-half; and when supper-time arrived he got rid of the rest. For the remainder of the journey he had nothing but the empty basket to carry, and the other Servants, whose loads seemed to get heavier and heavier at every step, could not but applaud his ingenuity.

Ingenuity lightens labor.

THE DEER AND THE LION

A Deer, being hard pressed by the Hounds, found a cave, into which he rushed for safety. An immense Lion, couched at the farther end of the cave, sprang upon him in an instant. "Unhappy creature that I am!" exclaimed the Stag, in his dying moments. "I entered this cave to escape the pursuit of Men and Dogs, and I have fallen into the jaws of the most terrible of wild Beasts."

In avoiding one evil, plunge not into a worse.

THE ASS' SHADOW

A Man, one hot day, hired an Ass, with his Driver, to carry some merchandise across a desert. The sun's rays were intensely hot and, unable to advance farther without a temporary rest, he called upon the Driver to stop, and proceeded to sit down in the Shadow of the Ass. The Driver, however, a lusty fellow, rudely pushed him away and sat down on the spot himself. "Nay, friend," said the Driver, "when you hired this Ass of me you said nothing about the Shadow. If now you want that too, you must pay for it." "But the Shadow goes with the Ass," replied the Man, "and both are my property." This the other disputed, and the quarrel waxing fiercer came to blows. While the men fought, the Ass sprang to its feet and galloped away.

Be sure of your bargains.

THE PASSENGER AND THE PILOT

It had blown a violent storm at sea, and the whole crew of a vessel were in imminent danger of shipwreck. After the rolling of the waves was somewhat abated, a certain Passenger who had never been to sea before, observing the Pilot to have appeared wholly unconcerned, even in their greatest danger, had the curiosity to ask him what death his father died. "What death?" said the Pilot; "why, he perished at sea, as my grandfather did before him." "And are you not afraid of trusting yourself to an element that has proved thus fatal to your family?" "Afraid? By no means; why, we must all die: is not your father dead?" "Yes, but he died in his bed." "And why, then, are you not afraid of trusting yourself in your bed?" "Because I am there perfectly secure." "It may be so," replied the Pilot; "but if the hand of Providence is equally extended over all places, there is no more reason for me to be afraid of going to sea than for you to be afraid of going to bed."

Faith is not a relative matter.

THE FOX AND THE CROW

A Crow, having stolen a piece of cheese from a cottage window, flew with it to a tree that was some way off. A Fox, drawn by the smell of the cheese, came and sat at the foot of the tree, and tried to find some way of making it his. "Good morning, dear Miss Crow," said he. "How well you are looking today! What handsome feathers yours are, to be sure! Perhaps, too, your voice is as sweet as your feathers are fine. If so, you are really the Queen of Birds." The Crow, quite beside herself to hear such praise, at once opened a wide beak to let the Fox judge of her voice, and so let fall the cheese. The Fox snapped it up, and exclaimed, "Ah! Ah! My good soul, learn that all who flatter have their own ends in view. That lesson will well repay you for a bit of cheese."

Beware the flatterer.

THE WOLF TEACHING THE FOX

Said the Fox to the Wolf, one day, "My friend, you have no idea how badly I often fare. A horribly tough old Cock, or a lean and shrivelled Hen, is a kind of food of which it is quite possible in time to get tired. Now, it seems to me that you live a good deal better than I do, and don't run into so much danger either. I have to go prowling about the houses: you get your prey in the fields. Teach me your business.

The Fox and the Crow

Let me be the first of my race to have a fat Sheep whenever I wish. Teach me, there's a good fellow, and you shall find yourself no loser in the end." "I will," said the Wolf; "and, by-the-by, I have just lost a brother. You will find his body over yonder. Slip into his skin, and come to me again." The Fox did as he was told, and the Wolf gave him many a lesson in growling, biting, fighting, and deportment, which the Fox executed first badly, then fairly, and in the end quite as well as his master. Just then a flock of Sheep came in sight, and into the midst of them rushed the new-made Wolf, with such fury and noise that Shepherd Boy, Dog, and Sheep fled in terror to gain their home, leaving only one poor Sheep behind, that had been seized by the throat. Just at that instant a Cock in the nearest farm crowed loud and shrill. There was no resisting the familiar sound. Out of the Wolf's skin slipped the Fox, and made towards the Cock as fast as he could, forgetting in a moment his lessons, the Sheep, the Professor, and everything else, about which he had just been making all the fuss in the world.

Training cannot overcome nature.

THE WOLF AND THE KID

A Wolf spied a Kid that had strayed to a distance from the herd, and pursued him. The Kid, finding that he could not escape, waited till the Wolf came up, and then assuming a cheerful tone, said, "I see clearly enough that I must be eaten, but I would fain die as pleasantly as I can. Give me, therefore, a few notes of the pipe you play so well, before I go to destruction." It seems that the Wolf was of a musical turn, and always carried his pipe with him. Flattered by the Kid's compliment, the Wolf played and the Kid danced, until the noise of the pipe brought the Dogs to the spot. The Wolf hastily fled, saying, "This is what comes when people will go meddling out of their profession. My business was to play the butcher, not the piper."

Stick to your task.

THE RAVEN AND THE SERPENT

A Hungry Raven, searching for prey, came across a Snake lying at full length on a sunny bank. He seized him in his horny beak and would have devoured him, but the Snake, twisting and turning about, bit the Raven with his venomous fangs, so that he died in great pain. "I am justly served," gasped the dying Bird, "for trying to profit by injuring another."

Have regard for the rights of others.

THE FOX AND THE LION

The first time the Fox saw the Lion he nearly died of fright. The next time, he gathered sufficient courage to have a good stare. The third time, he went boldly up to the Lion, and commenced a familiar conversation with him.

Familiarity breeds contempt.

THE HEN AND THE FOX

A Fox, having crept into a henhouse, looked up and down for something to eat, and at last spied a Hen sitting upon a perch so high, that he could by no means reach her. He therefore had recourse to an old stratagem. "Dear cousin," said he to her, "how do you do? I heard that you were ill, and kept at home; I could not rest, therefore, till I had come to see you. Pray let me feel your pulse. Indeed, you do not look well at all." He was running on in this impudent manner, when the Hen answered him from the roost, "Truly, dear Fox, you are in the right. I was seldom in more danger than I am now. Pray excuse my coming down; I am sure I should catch my death if I were to." The Fox, finding himself foiled, made off and tried his luck elsewhere.

Craft can be answered with craft.

THE FOX AND THE COCK

A Fox, passing early one summer's morning near a farmyard, was caught in a trap which the farmer had planted there for that purpose. A Cock saw at a distance what had happened, and hardly daring to trust himself too near so dangerous a foe, approached him cautiously and peeped at him, not without considerable fear. The Fox saw him, and in his most bewitching manner addressed him as follows: "See, dear cousin," said he, "what an unfortunate accident has befallen me here! And, believe me, it is all on your account. I was creeping through yonder hedge, on my way homeward, when I heard you crow, and resolved, before I went any farther, to come and ask after your health. On the way I met with this disaster. Now if you would but run to the house and bring me a pointed stick, I think I could force it into this trap and free myself from its grip. Such a service, believe me, I should not soon forget." The Cock ran off and soon came back, not without the stick. But it was carried in the hand of the sturdy farmer, to whom he had told the story, and who lost no time in putting it out of Master Fox's power to do any harm for the future.

Use discrimination in your charities.

THE FORTUNE-TELLER

A Man who gave himself out as a Wizard and Fortune-teller used to stand in the marketplace and pretend to foretell the future, give information as to missing property, and other matters of the like kind. One day, while he was busily plying his trade, a waggish fellow broke through the crowd, and gasping as if for want of breath, told him that his house was in flames, and must shortly be burnt to the ground. Off ran the Wizard at the news as fast as his legs could carry him, while the Wag and a crowd of other people followed at his heels. But the house was not on fire at all; and the Wag asked him, amid the jeers of the people, how it was that he, who was so clever at telling other people's fortunes, should know so little of his own.

'Tis a poor baker who will not eat his own wares.

THE FARMER AND HIS THREE ENEMIES

A Wolf, a Fox, and a Hare happened to be foraging, one evening, in different parts of a farm. Their first effort was pretty successful, and they returned in safety to their several quarters; however, not so happy as to be unperceived by the Farmer's watchful eye, who, placing several kinds of snares, made each of them his prisoner in the next attempt. He first took the Hare to task, who confessed she had eaten a few turnip-tops, merely to satisfy her hunger; besought him piteously to spare her life; and promised never to enter his grounds again. He then accosted the Fox, who, in a fawning, obsequious tone, protested that he came into his premises through no other motive than pure good nature, to restrain the Hares and other vermin from the plunder of his corn; and that, whatever evil tongues might say, he had too great a regard both for him and justice to be in the least capable of any dishonest action. He last of all examined the Wolf, as to the business that brought him. The Wolf boldly declared that it was with a view of destroying his Lambs, to which he had an undoubted right; that the Farmer himself was the only felon, who robbed the community of Wolves of what was meant to be their proper food. That this, at least, was his opinion; and whatever fate attended him, he should not scruple to risk his life in the pursuit of his lawful prey. The Farmer, having heard their pleas, determined the cause in the following manner: "The Hare," said he, "deserves compassion for the penitence she shows, and the humble confession she has made. As for the Fox and the Wolf, let them be hanged together; their crimes deserve it, and are heightened by their hypocrisy and impudence."

The wrongdoer can obtain forgiveness most easily by confessing his sin.

THE FROG AND THE FOX

A Frog came out of his native marsh, and, hopping to the top of a mound of earth, gave out to all the Beasts around that he was a great physician, and could heal all manner of diseases. The Fox demanded

The Frog and the Fox

why, if he was so clever, he did not mend his own blotched and spotted body, his stare eyes, and his lantern jaws.

Physician, heal thyself.

THE MULES AND THE ROBBERS

Two Mules were being driven along a lonely road. One was laden with Corn and the other with Gold. The one that carried the Gold was so proud of his burden that, although it was very heavy, he would not for the world have the least bit of it taken away. He trotted along with stately step, his bells jingling as he went. By-and-by, some Robbers fell upon them. They let the Mule that carried the Corn go free; but they seized the Gold which the other carried, and, as he kicked and struggled to prevent their robbing him, they stabbed him to the heart. In dying, he said to the other Mule, "I see, brother, it is not always well to have grand duties to perform. If, like you, I had only served a Miller, this sad state would not now be mine."

Do not flatter yourself simply because you carry a little gold.

SOCRATES AND HIS FRIENDS

Socrates once built a house, and everybody who saw it had something or other to say against it. "What a front!" said one. "What an inside!" said another. "What rooms! Not big enough to turn round in," said a third. "Small as it is," answered Socrates, "I wish I had true Friends enough to fill it."

Houses are easier to get than friends.

THE OLD WOMAN AND THE CASK

An Old Woman found an empty Cask which had lately been full of prime old Wine, and which still retained the smell of its former contents. She greedily placed it several times to her nose, and sniffing it with a sigh, said: "O most delicious! How nice must the Wine itself have been, when it leaves so sweet a perfume!"

The memory of a good deed lives on.

THE GARDENER AND HIS LANDLORD

A simple sort of Gardener, who rented a cottage and small garden on the outskirts of a park belonging to a great Squire, was much annoyed at the havoc that a certain Hare made with his choice and delicate young vegetables. So off went the Man one morning to complain to the Squire. "This Hare," said he, "laughs at all snares. He has a charm that keeps off all the sticks and stones that I throw at him. In plain truth, I believe he is no Hare at all, but a wizard in disguise." "Nay, were he the father of all wizards," replied the Squire, who was a great hunter, "my Dogs will make short work with him. We'll come tomorrow, and see about it." The next morning came the Squire with his pack of Hounds, and a score of friends, huntsmen and others. The Gardener was at breakfast, and felt bound to ask them to partake. They did so and made great inroads upon his store of provisions. "Now, then, let us beat for the Hare," cried the Squire; and the huntsmen blew their horns with deafening noise, and the Dogs flew here and there in search of the Hare, who was soon started from under a big cabbage where he had gone for shelter. Across the garden ran the Hare, and after him went the Dogs. Alas for the beds, the frames, the flowers! Through the hedge went the Hare, and over the beds and through the hedge after him went the Squire, the friends, the huntsmen, horses and all. A wreck indeed did the place look, when they were gone. "Ah!" cried the Gardener, "fool that I was to go to the great for help! Here is more damage done in half an hour than all the Hares in the province would have made in a year!"

Do not ask others to do what you can do yourself.

THE HORSE AND THE HOG

A Hog that was lazily lying in the sun saw a Warhorse advancing, on his way to the battlefield. The Warhorse was gaily caparisoned, and proudly spurned the ground, as if impatient to charge the enemy. The Hog half lifted his head and, grunting, said to him, "What a fool you are to be so ready to rush to your death!" "Your speech," replied the Horse, "fits well a vile animal, that only lives to get fat and be killed by the knife. If I die on the field, I die where duty calls me, and I shall leave the memory of a good name behind."

'Tis not death but the manner of it which is important.

THE SATYR AND THE TRAVELER[5]

A Satyr, ranging in the forest in winter, came across a Traveler half starved and nearly dead with the cold. He took pity on him and invited him to go to his cave. On their way the Man kept blowing upon his fingers. "Why do you do that?" said the Satyr, who had seen little of the world. "To warm my hands; they are nearly frozen," replied the Man. Arrived at the cave, the Satyr poured out a mess of smoking pottage and laid it before the Traveler, who commenced to blow at it with all his might. "What, blowing again!" cried the Satyr. "Is it not hot enough?" "Yes, faith," answered the Man, "it is too hot. I am blowing at it to cool it off." "Be off with you!" said the Satyr, in alarm; "I will have no part with a Man who can blow hot and cold from the same mouth."

A two-faced man makes no friends.

THE OLD TROUT, THE YOUNG TROUT, AND THE SALMON

A Fisherman, in the month of May, stood angling on the bank of a river with an artificial fly. He threw his bait with so much art that a Young Trout was rushing towards it, when she was prevented by her mother. "Stop, child!" said she, "never be too hasty where there is a possibility of danger. Take due time to consider, before you risk an action that may be fatal. How do you know whether that is indeed a fly, or the snare of an enemy? Let someone else make the experiment before you. If it be a fly, he will very probably elude the first attack, and then the second may be made, if not with success, at least with safety." She had no sooner uttered this caution than a Salmon seized upon the pretended fly, and was captured.

Do not rush into a strange position.

THE CAT AND THE FOX

The Cat and the Fox were once talking together in the middle of a forest. "Let things be never so bad," said the Fox, "I don't care; I have a hundred tricks to escape my enemies, if one should fail." "I," replied the Cat, "have but one; if that fails me, I am undone." "I am sorry for you," said the Fox. "You are truly to be pitied; and if you were not such a helpless creature, I'd give you one or two of my tricks. As it is, I suppose each must shift for himself." Just then a pack of Hounds burst into view. The Cat, having recourse to her one means of defense, flew up a tree, and sat securely among the branches, from whence she saw the Fox, after trying his hundred tricks in vain, overtaken by the Dogs and torn in pieces.

One thing well learned brings safety.

THE FOX, THE WOLF, AND THE HORSE

A Fox seeing a Horse for the first time, grazing in a field, at once ran to a Wolf of his acquaintance, and described the animal that he had found. "It is, perhaps," said the Fox, "some delicious prey that fortune has put in our path. Come with me, and judge for yourself." Off they ran, and soon came to the Horse, who, scarcely lifting his head, seemed little anxious to be on speaking terms with such suspicious-looking characters. "Sir," said the Fox, "your humble servants wish to learn the name by which you are known to your illustrious friends." The Horse, who was not without a ready wit, replied that his name had been curiously written upon his hoofs for the information of those who cared to read it. "Gladly would I," replied the sly Fox, suspecting in an instant something wrong, "but my parents were poor, and could not pay for my education: hence, I never learned to read. The family of my companion here, on the contrary, are great folk, and he can both read and write, and has a thousand other accomplishments." The Wolf, pleased with the flattery, at once went up, with a knowing air, to examine one of the hoofs which the Horse raised for his convenience; and when he had come near enough, the Horse gave a sudden and vigorous kick, and back to earth fell the Wolf, his jaw broken and bleeding. "Well, cousin," cried the Fox, with a grin, "you need never ask for the name a second time, now that you have it written so plainly just below your eyes."

Curiosity and conceit come to grief.

JUPITER'S TWO WALLETS

When Jupiter made Man, he gave him two Wallets—one for his neighbor's faults, the other for his own. He threw them over the Man's shoulder, so that one hung in front and the other behind. The Man kept the one in front for his neighbor's faults, and the one behind for his own; so that while the first was always under his nose, it took some pains to see the latter. This custom, which began thus early, is not quite unknown at the present day.

One can always see his neighbor's faults more easily than his own.

THE FOX AND THE HEDGEHOG[6]

A Fox, swimming across a river, was drifted along by the stream, and carried by an eddy into a nook on the opposite bank. He lay there exhausted, and unable for a time to scramble up. To add to his misfortunes a swarm of Flies settled upon his head, and stung and plagued him grievously. A Hedgehog that happened to be near the edge of the water offered to drive away the Flies that molested and teased him in that sad manner. "Nay," cried the Fox, "pray let them alone. Those that are now upon me are already full almost to bursting with my blood. If you drive them away, a fresh swarm of hungry rascals will take their places, and I shall not have a drop of blood left in my body."

Old trials are better borne than new ones.

A BOAR CHALLENGES AN ASS

Some hard words passed between a Boar and an Ass, and a challenge followed upon them. The Boar, priding himself upon his tusks, and comparing his head with the Ass' head, looked forward to the fight with confidence. The time for the battle came. The combatants approached one another. The Boar rushed upon the Ass, who, suddenly turning round, let his hoofs fly with all his might right in the jaws of the Boar, so that the latter staggered and fell back. "Well," said he, "who could have expected an attack from that end?"

Attacks come from unexpected quarters.

THE WOLF AND THE MASTIFF[7]

A Wolf, who was almost skin and bone—so well did the Dogs of the neighborhood keep guard—met, one moonshiny night, a sleek Mastiff, who was, moreover, as strong as he was fat. The Wolf would gladly have supped off him, but saw there would first be a great fight, for which, in his condition, he was not prepared; so, bidding the Dog goodnight very humbly, he praised his good looks. "It would be easy for you," replied the Mastiff, "to get as fat as I am, if you liked. Quit this forest, where you and your fellows live so wretchedly, and often

The Wolf and the Mastiff

die with hunger. Follow me, and you shall fare much better." "What shall I have to do?" asked the Wolf. "Almost nothing," answered the Dog; "only chase away the beggars, and fawn upon the folks of the house. You will, in return, be paid with all sorts of nice things—bones of fowls and pigeons—to say nothing of many a friendly pat on the head." The Wolf, at the picture of so much comfort, nearly shed tears of joy. They trotted off together, but, as they went along, the Wolf noticed a bare spot on the Dog's neck. "What is that mark?" said he. "Oh, nothing," said the Dog. "How nothing?" urged the Wolf. "Just the merest trifle," answered the Dog; "the collar which I wear when I am tied up is the cause of it." "Tied up!" exclaimed the Wolf, with a sudden stop; "tied up! Can you not always, then, run where you please?" "Well, not quite always," said the Mastiff; "but what can that matter?" "It matters so much to me," rejoined the Wolf, "that your lot shall not be mine at any price"; and leaping away, he ran once more to his native forest.

Liberty is priceless.

THE NIGHTINGALE AND HIS CAGE[7]

A Nightingale, which belonged to a person of quality, was fed every day with plenty of choice dainties, and kept in a stately cage. Yet, notwithstanding this happy condition, he was uneasy, and envied the condition of those birds who lived free in the woods, and hopped up and down, unconfined, from bough to bough. He earnestly longed to lead the same life, and secretly pined because his wishes were denied him. After some time, however, it happened that the door of his cage was left unfastened, and the long-wished-for opportunity was given him of making his escape. Accordingly, out he flew, and hid himself among the shades of a neighboring wood, where he thought to spend the remainder of his days in contentment. But, alas! The poor bird was mistaken; a thousand evils which he never dreamed of attended this elopement of his, and he was now really that miserable creature which before he had been only in imagination. The delicate food that he used to eat was no more; he did not know how to provide for himself, and was even ready to die with hunger. A storm of rain, thunder, and lightning filled all the air, and he had no place of safety; his feathers were wetted with the heavy shower, and he was almost blinded with the flashes of lightning. His tender nature could not withstand the severe shock; he even died under it. But just before he breathed his last he is said to have made this reflection: "Ah, were I but in my cage again, I would never wander more."

Liberty is most attractive to those who do not know its price.

THE APE AND THE BEE

An Ape, who, having a great desire to partake of the honey which was deposited in a rich Beehive, but was intimidated from meddling with it by having felt the smart of the sting, made the following reflection: "How strange, that a Bee, while producing a delicacy so passing sweet and tempting, should also carry with him a sting so dreadfully bitter!" "Yes," answered the Bee, "equal to the sweetness of my better work is the bitterness of my sting when my anger is provoked."

Beware how you arouse the little man.

THE WOLF AND THE FOX

The Wolves and Foxes once selected one of their number to be their ruler. The Wolf that was chosen was a plausible, smooth-spoken rascal, and on a very early day he addressed an assembly of his subjects as follows: "One thing," he said, "is of such vital importance, and will tend so much to our general welfare, that I cannot impress it too strongly upon your attention. Nothing cherishes true brotherly feeling and promotes the general good so much as the suppression of all selfishness. Let each one of you, then, share with any hungry brother who may be near whatever in hunting may fall to your lot." "Hear, hear!" cried a Fox, who had listened to the speech; "and of course you yourself will begin with the fat Sheep that you hid yesterday in a corner of your lair."

Practice what you preach.

THE YOUNG MOUSE, THE COCK, AND THE CAT

A Young Mouse, on his return to his hole after leaving it for the first time, thus recounted his adventures to his mother. "Mother," said he, "quitting this narrow place where you have brought me up, I rambled about today like a Mouse of spirit, who wished to see and to be seen, when two such notable creatures came in my way! One was so gracious, so gentle and benign! The other, who was just as noisy and forbidding, had on his head and under his chin, pieces of raw meat, which shook at every step he took; and then, all at once, beating his sides with the utmost fury, he uttered such a harsh and piercing cry that I fled in terror; and this, too, just as I was about to introduce myself to the other stranger, who was covered with fur like our own, only richer-looking and much more beautiful, and who seemed so modest and benevolent that it did my heart good to look at her." "Ah, my son," replied the Old Mouse, "learn while you live to distrust appearances. The first strange creature was nothing but a Fowl, that will ere long be killed, and off his bones, when put on a dish in the pantry, we may make a delicious supper; while the other was a nasty, sly, and bloodthirsty hypocrite of a Cat, to whom no food is so welcome as a young and juicy little Mouse like yourself."

Do not trust appearances.

THE BEAR AND THE FOX

The Bear is said to be unwilling to touch the dead body of a man; and one of the animals was once heard making a virtue of this peculiarity. "Such is my regard for mankind," said he, "that nothing on earth would induce me to injure a human corpse." "Your kindness would impress me much more," said a Fox who was listening to this speech, "if I could believe that you paid the same respect to the living that you profess to do to the dead."

Regard is not shown in half-service.

THE ASS IN THE LION'S SKIN

An Ass once found the skin of a Lion, put it on, and was highly amused to note how his presence brought terror to the other animals wherever he went. In his delight he could not resist raising his voice and braying loudly. At the sound, a Fox, who had been skulking off, turned about and said: "Ah, I thought you were a Lion, too, until I heard you bray."

Clothes do not make the man.

JUPITER AND THE ANIMALS

Jupiter, one day being in great good-humor, called upon all living things to come before him, and if, looking at themselves and at one another, there should be in the appearance of any one of them anything which admitted of improvement, they were to speak of it without fear. "Come, Master Ape," said he, "you shall speak first. Look around you, and then say, are you satisfied with your good looks?" "I should think so," answered the Ape; "and have I not reason? If I were clumsy like my brother the Bear, now, I might have something to say." "Nay," growled the Bear, "I don't see that there's much to find fault with in me; but if you could manage to lengthen the tail and trim the ears of our friend the Elephant, that might be an improvement." The Elephant, in his turn, said that he had always considered the Whale a great deal too big to be comely. The Ant thought the Mite so small as to be beneath notice. Jupiter became angry to witness so much conceit, and sent them all about their business.

Think not of yourself more highly than of your neighbors.

The Thief and the Dog

THE THIEF AND THE DOG

A Thief who came near a house one night to rob it, was prevented by a Dog who began to bark loudly. The Thief tried to coax him into silence by offering him a tempting piece of meat. "No," said the Dog, "I will not sell my Master and myself for a bite of meat. For, after you have finished with him, who will take care of me?"

Honesty is the best policy.

HERCULES AND STRIFE

Hercules, once journeying along a narrow roadway, came across a strange-looking animal that reared its head and threatened him. Undaunted, the hero gave him a few lusty blows with his club, and thought to have gone on his way. The monster however, much to the astonishment of Hercules, was now three times as big as it was before, and of a still more threatening aspect. He thereupon redoubled his blows and laid about him fast and furiously; but the harder and quicker the strokes of the club, the bigger and more frightful grew the monster, which now completely filled up the road. Pallas[8] then appeared upon the scene. "Stop, Hercules," said she. "Cease your blows. The monster's name is Strife. Let it alone, and it will soon become as little as it was at first."

Strife increases with turmoil.

THE OLD LION

A Lion, worn out with age, lay drawing his last breath, and several of the Beasts who had formerly been sufferers by him came and revenged themselves. The Boar, with his powerful tusks, ripped his flank; and the Bull gored his sides with his horns. The Ass, too, seeing there was no danger, came up and threw his heels into the Lion's face. "Alas!"

The Old Lion

groaned the dying tyrant, "how much worse than a thousand deaths it is to be spurned by so base a creature."

Respect earns respect.

TWO TRAVELERS OF DIFFERING HUMORS

There were two Men of very different humors together upon a journey. One went despondingly on, with a thousand cares and troubles in his head, exclaiming every now and then, "Whatever shall I do to live!" The other jogged merrily along, determined to keep a good heart, to do his best, and leave the issue to Fortune. "How can you be so merry?" said the Sorrowful plodder. "As I am a sinner, my heart is ready to break, for fear I should want bread." "Tut, Man!" said the other, "there's enough bread and to spare for all of us." Presently the Grumbler had another heavy thought that made him groan aloud. "What a dreadful thing it would be if I were struck blind!" said he, and he must needs walk on ahead with his eyes shut, to try how it would seem if that misfortune should befall him. His Fellow-traveler, coming after him, picked up a purse of gold which the other, having his eyes shut, had not perceived; and thus was he punished for his mistrust, for the purse had been his, if he had not first willingly put it out of his power to see it.

Fortune helps those who help themselves.

THE TRAVELERS AND THE OYSTER

As two Men were walking by the seaside at low water, they saw an Oyster, and both stooped at the same time to pick it up. One pushed the other away, and a dispute ensued. A third Traveler coming along at the time, they determined to refer the matter to him, which of the two had the better right to the Oyster. While each was telling his story, the Arbitrator gravely took out his knife, opened the Shell, and loosened the Oyster. When they had finished, and were listening for his decision, he just as gravely swallowed the Oyster, and offered them each a Shell. "The Court," said he, "awards you each a Shell. The Oyster will cover the costs."

Those who seek justice must pay for it.

THE CROW AND THE MUSSEL

A Crow, having found a Mussel on the seashore, took it in his beak, and tried for a long time to break the shell by hammering it upon a stone. Another Crow—a sly old fellow—came and watched him for some time in silence. "Friend," said he at last, "you'll never break it in that way. Listen to me. This is the way to do it: Fly up as high as you can, and let the thing fall upon a rock. It will be smashed then, sure enough, and you can eat it at your leisure." The simpleminded Crow did as he was told, flew up and let the Mussel fall. Before he could descend to eat it, however, the other Bird had pounced upon it and carried it away.

Beware of interested advisers.

THE CROW AND THE PITCHER

A Crow, ready to die with thirst, flew with joy to a Pitcher, hoping to find some water in it. He found some there, to be sure, but only a little drop at the bottom, which he was quite unable to reach. He then tried to overturn the Pitcher, but it was too heavy. So he gathered up some pebbles, with which the ground was covered, and, taking them one by one in his beak, dropped them into the Pitcher. By this means the water gradually reached the top, and he was able to drink at his ease.

Necessity is the mother of invention.

THE SHEPHERD AND THE YOUNG WOLF

A Shepherd found the young Cub of a Wolf, and caused it to be brought up among his Dogs, with whom it grew to be quite friendly. When any other Wolves came, meaning to rob the fold, this young fellow was among the foremost to give them chase, but on returning he generally managed to linger behind the Dogs, and keep a sharp lookout for any stray Sheep from the fold. Instead, however, of bringing these home, he would drive them to an out-of-the-way spot, and there mangle and partially devour them. He did this once too often, and was caught at it by the Shepherd, who hung him by the neck from the bough of a tree, and in that way put an end to his double-dealing.

Double-dealing is worse than open enmity.

THE CLOWNS AND THE PIG

On the occasion of some festivities that were given by a Roman nobleman, a certain droll Clown caused much laughter by his tricks upon the stage, and, more than all, by his imitation of the squeaking of a Pig. It seemed to the hearers so real, that they called for it again and again. One Man, however, in the audience, thought the imitation was not perfect; and he made his way to the stage, and said that if he were permitted, he tomorrow would enter the lists, and squeak against the Clown for a wager. The mob, anticipating great fun, shouted their consent, and accordingly, when the next day came, the two rival Jokers were in their place. The hero of the previous day went first, and the hearers, more pleased than ever, fairly roared with delight. Then came the turn of the other who, having a Pig carefully concealed under his cloak so that no one would have suspected its existence, vigorously pinched its ear with his thumbnail, and made it squeak with a vengeance. "Not half as good—not half as good!" cried the audience, and many among them even began to hiss. "Fine judges you!" replied the Man, drawing the Pig from under his cloak, and showing it to them. "Behold the performer that you condemn!"

A prejudiced jury is hard to convince.

THE HORSE AND THE GROOM

A Dishonest Groom used regularly to sell a good half of the measure of oats that was daily allowed for a Horse, the care of which was entrusted to him. He would, however, keep currying the animal for hours together, to make him appear in good condition. The Horse naturally resented this treatment. "If you really wish me to look sleek," said he, "in future give me half the currying, and twice as much food."

There is no parleying with the dishonest.

THE MAID AND THE PAIL OF MILK

A Milkmaid, having been a good girl for a long time, and careful in her work, her mistress gave her a Pail of New Milk for herself. With the Pail on her head, she was tripping gaily along to the house of the doctor, who was going to give a large party, and wanted the Milk. "For this Milk," thought she, as she went, "I shall get enough money to buy twenty of the eggs laid by our neighbor's fine fowls. These eggs I shall put under mistress' old hen, and if only half of the chicks grow up and thrive before the next fair time comes round, I shall be able to sell them for enough to buy a new gown, with maybe enough left to get that jacket I saw in the village the other day, and a hat and ribbons too, and when I go to the fair how smart I shall be! All the Young Fellows will notice me, but when they come around, I shall just toss my head and——" Here the Maid gave her head the toss she was thinking about. Down came the Pail, and the Milk ran out on the ground! Good-bye now to eggs, chicken, gown, jacket, hat, ribbons, and all!

Do not count your chickens before they are hatched.

THE LION AND THE FOUR BULLS

Four Bulls were such great friends that they always kept together when feeding. A Lion watched them for many days with longing eyes; but never being able to find one apart from the rest, was afraid to

The Lion and the Four Bulls

attack them. He at length succeeded in awakening a jealousy among them, which finally became hatred, and they strayed off at some distance from each other. The Lion then fell upon them singly, and killed them all.

There is strength in unity.

THE CAT AND THE SPARROWS

A great friendship once existed between a Sparrow and a Cat, to whom, when quite a kitten, the Bird had been given. When they were playing together, the bold Sparrow would often fly into little mimic rages, and peck the Cat with his bill, while Pussy would beat him off with only half-opened claws; and though this sport would often wax warm, there was never real anger between them. It happened, however, that the Bird made the acquaintance of another Sparrow, and being both of them saucy fellows, they soon fell out and quarreled in earnest. The little friend of the Cat, in these fights, generally fared the worst; and one day he came trembling all over with passion, and besought the Cat to avenge his wrongs for him. Pussy thereupon pounced on the offending stranger, and speedily crunched him up and swallowed him. "I had no idea before that Sparrows were so nice," said the Cat to herself, for her blood was now stirred; and as quick as thought her little playmate was seized and sent to join his enemy.

Trouble is more easily started than stopped.

THE MILLER, HIS SON, AND THEIR ASS

A Miller and his Son were driving their Ass to a neighboring fair to sell him. They had not gone far when they met with a troop of women collected round a well, talking and laughing. "Look there," cried one of them, "did you ever see such fellows, to be trudging along the road on foot when they might ride?" The Miller hearing this, quickly made his Son mount the Ass, and continued to walk along merrily by his side. Presently they came up to a group of old men in earnest debate. "There," said one of them, "it proves what I was a-saying. What respect is shown to old age in these days? Do you see that idle lad riding while his old father has to walk? Get down, you young scapegrace, and let the old man rest his weary limbs." Upon this, the Miller made his Son dismount, and got up himself. In this manner they had not proceeded far when they met a company of women and children. "Why, you lazy old fellow," cried several tongues at once, "how can you ride upon the beast, while that poor little lad there can hardly keep pace by the side of you?" The good-natured Miller immediately took up his Son behind him. They had now almost reached the town. "Pray, honest friend," said a citizen, "is that Ass your own?" "Yes," replied the old man. "O, one would not have thought so," said the other, "by the way you load him. Why, you two fellows are better able to carry the poor beast than he you." "Anything to please you," said the Miller; "we can but try." So, alighting with his Son, they tied the legs of the Ass together, and by the help of a pole endeavored to carry him on their shoulders over a bridge near the entrance of the town. This entertaining sight brought the people in crowds to laugh at it; till the Ass, not liking the noise, nor the strange handling that he was subject to, broke the cords that bound him, and, tumbling off the pole, fell into the river. Upon this, the old man, vexed and ashamed, made the best of his way home again, convinced that by trying to please everybody he had pleased nobody, and lost his Ass into the bargain.

He who tries to please everybody pleases nobody.

THE SHEPHERD TURNED MERCHANT

A Shepherd who kept his Sheep at no great distance from the sea one day drove them close to the shore, and sat down on a rock to enjoy the cool breeze. It was a beautiful summer day, and the ocean lay before him, calm, smooth, and of an enchanting blue. As he watched the white sails, and listened to the measured splash of the tiny wavelets on the pebbled beach, his heart thrilled with pleasure. "How happy," exclaimed he, "should I be if, in a tight, trim bark of my own, with wings like a bird, I could skim that lovely plain, visit other lands, see other peoples, and become rich in ministering to their wants and pleasures!" He sold his flock, and all that he had, bought a small ship, loaded her with dates, and set sail. A storm arose: the cargo was thrown overboard to lighten the ship, but in spite of all efforts she was driven upon a rock near the shore, and went to pieces. The Shepherd narrowly escaped with his life, and was afterwards glad to earn his bread by watching the flock which had formerly been his own. In the course of time, when, by care and frugality, he had again become possessed of some amount of wealth, he happened to find himself sitting on the self-same rock, and on just such another lovely day as that on which he had resolved to become a Merchant. The sea lapped temptingly on the beach at his feet. "Foolish Sea!" the Shepherd cried, "do you think I am ass enough to try you a second time? You want some more dates, do you?"

Experience is a sure teacher.

THE HARE AFRAID OF HIS EARS

The Lion, being once badly hurt by the horns of a Goat, went into a great rage, and swore that every animal with horns should be banished from his kingdom. Goats, Bulls, Rams, Deer, and every living thing with horns had quickly to be off on pain of death. A Hare, seeing from his shadow how long his ears were, was in great fear lest they should be taken for horns. "Goodbye, my friend," said he to a Cricket who, for many a long summer evening, had chirped to him where he lay dozing: "I must be off from here. My ears are too much like horns to allow me to be comfortable." "Horns!" exclaimed the Cricket, "do you take me for a fool? You no more have horns than I have." "Say what you please," replied the Hare, "were my ears only half as long as they are, they would be quite long enough for anyone to lay hold of who wished to make them out to be horns."

Avoid the appearance of evil.

THE HARE AND THE DOG

A Dog once gave a long chase to a Hare. The Dog, having not long since made a good meal, was not at all hungry, and in consequence in no hurry to put an end to the sport. He would at times, as they ran, snap at the Hare, and at others lick him with his tongue. "Pray," cried the persecuted and bewildered Hare, "are you a friend or an enemy? If a friend, why do you bite me so? And if an enemy, why caress me?"

Open enmity is better than doubtful friendship.

THE GRATEFUL EAGLE AND THE FOX

A Man caught an Eagle in a snare, cut his wings close, and kept him chained to a stump in his yard. A kind-hearted Fowler, seeing the melancholy looking bird, took pity on him, and bought him. He was now well treated, and his wings were allowed to grow. When they had grown again sufficiently for him to fly, the Fowler gave him his liberty. The first thing the Bird caught was a fine fat Hare, which he brought and gratefully laid at the feet of his benefactor. A Fox, looking on, said that he would have done better to try to make friends with the first Man who had caught him, and who might, perhaps, catch him yet again, rather than with the second, from whom he had nothing to fear. "Your advice may do very well for a Fox," replied the Eagle; "but it is my nature to serve those who have been kind to me, rather than be governed by fear."

Fear commands poorer service than kindness.

THE BEE AND THE FLY

A Bee observing a Fly frisking about her hive, asked him in a very angry tone what he did there. "Is it for such fellows as you," said she, "to intrude into the company of the queens of the air?" "You have great reason, truly," replied the Fly, "to be out of humor. I am sure they must

be mad who would have any concern with so quarrelsome a nation."
"And why so, may I ask?" returned the enraged Bee. "We have the best
laws and are governed by the best policy in the world. We feed upon the
most fragrant flowers, and all our business is to make honey; honey,
which equals nectar, low, tasteless wretch, who live upon nothing but
vile things." "We live as we can," rejoined the Fly. "Poverty, I hope, is no
crime; but passion is one, I am sure. The honey you make is sweet, I
grant you, but your heart is all bitterness; for to be revenged on an
enemy you will destroy your own life, and are so foolish in your rage as
to do more mischief to yourselves than to your enemy. Take my word
for it, one had better have fewer talents, and use them more wisely."

Well governed communities should make well governed individuals.

THE THRESHER AND THE EAR OF CORN

It once happened that an Ear of Corn, which lay under the heavy
blows of a Thresher's flail, thus expressed its sense of the unaccount-
able hard treatment: "How have I deserved this severe persecution?
Do I not appear before you in the simple covering which Nature gave
me; and although mankind freely acknowledge me as their greatest
blessing, you treat me as if I had been their curse." "Fool that thou
art!" replied the Thresher, when he heard the complaint; "know that
by this very treatment your value and your power of blessing is infi-
nitely increased, and that by it you are divested and freed from a
worthless excrescence, and are made more pure."

Punishments inflicted with discretion become wholesome correction.

THE FIR TREE AND THE BRAMBLE

The Fir Tree treated with contempt the Bramble that grew at its foot.
"I am put to many high and noble uses," said he boastfully. "I furnish
taper spars for ships, and beams for the roofs of palaces. You are

The Fir Tree and the Bramble

trodden under foot, and despised by everybody." "You talk very finely now," replied the Bramble; "but, for all that, when once you feel the axe applied to your root, you'll wish you had been a Bramble."

Better poverty without care than riches with care.

THE CRAB AND THE FOX

A Crab, forsaking the seashore, chose a neighboring green meadow as its feeding ground. A Fox came across him, and being very much famished ate him up. Just as he was on the point of being eaten, the Crab said, "I well deserve my fate; for what business had I on the land, when by my nature and habits I am only adapted for the sea?"

Contentment with our lot is an element of happiness.

THE EAGLE AND THE ARROW

An Eagle sat on a lofty rock intently watching a Hare whom he intended presently to pounce upon. An Archer, taking advantage of the Eagle's carelessness, aimed an arrow at him, and wounded him mortally. The Eagle gave one look at the death-dealing arrow and saw that it carried one of his own feathers. "Bitter it is to die!" he exclaimed; "but doubly bitter to have helped speed the cause of my death!"

Our misfortunes bite the keener when we have brought them on ourselves.

JUPITER'S LOTTERY

Jupiter, in order to please mankind, directed Mercury to give notice that he had established a lottery, in which there were no blanks; and that amongst a variety of other valuable chances, wisdom was the highest prize. It was Jupiter's command that in this lottery some of the gods should also become adventurers. The tickets being disposed of, and the wheels placed, Mercury was employed to preside at the drawing. It happened that the best prize fell to Minerva, upon which a general murmur ran through the assembly, and hints were thrown out that Jupiter had used some unfair practices to secure this desirable lot to his daughter. Jupiter, that he might at once punish and silence these impious clamors of the human race, presented them with folly in the place of wisdom; with which they went away perfectly well contented. From that time the greatest fools have always looked upon themselves as the wisest men.

Folly, passing with men for wisdom, makes each contented with his own share of understanding.

HERCULES AND PLUTUS

When Hercules was raised to the dignity of a god, and took his place on Olympus, he went round and paid his respects to all the gods and goddesses, excepting only Plutus, the god of Wealth, to whom he made no sign. This caused much astonishment, and Jupiter, at the first favorable opportunity, asked Hercules for an explanation. "Why," answered he, "I have seen that god in the company of such rascals when on earth, that I did not know whether it would be considered reputable to be seen talking to him in heaven."

Wealth and respectability are often at variance.

THE MOTHER, THE NURSE, AND THE FAIRY

One morning a mother entered the nursery to take up her newborn son and there found the Nurse wringing her hands in distress. "O my Lady!" sobbed the nurse. "Disaster has surely befallen your son. Some time in the night, invisible Fairies spirited him away and left in his place a hideous changeling. See how the child whose features once were the mirror of his parents' beauty now reflects the image of the fool." Just then a tiny Fairy popped through the keyhole swift as light and, perched upon the cradle top, upbraided the Nurse thusly: "Whence this conceit that the Fairy-folk supplies the world with fools which we freely give away. Like you, we dote upon our children. Wherever yet was found a mother who would give up her own flesh and blood. Were we to exchange ourselves for you dull sons of clay, then we might pass for fools indeed!"

To the vain, the greatest fault is that others do not resemble them.

THE MOCKINGBIRD

There is a certain Bird in America which has the faculty of mimicking the notes of every other songster, without being able himself to add any original strains to the concert. One of these Mockingbirds displayed his talent of ridicule among the branches of a venerable wood. "'Tis very well," said a little warbler, speaking for all the rest; "we grant you that our music is not without its faults; but why will you not favor us with a strain of your own?"

Many ridicule the things that they themselves cannot do.

THE BOYS AND THE FROGS

Some Boys, playing near a pond, saw a number of Frogs in the water, and began to pelt them with stones. They killed several of them, when one of the Frogs, lifting his head out of the water, cried out: "Pray stop, my boys: what is sport to you, is death to us."

There are two sides to every question.

THE BEGGAR AND HIS DOG

A Beggar and his Dog sat at the gate of a noble courtier, and were preparing to make a meal on a bowl of fragments that had been brought out by the kitchen-maid. A poor dependant of his Lordship's, who had been sharing the singular favor of a dinner at the steward's table, was struck with the appearance, and stopped a little to observe them. The Beggar, hungry and voracious as any courtier in Christendom, seized with greediness the choicest morsels and swallowed them himself; the residue was divided into portions for his children. A scrag was thrust into one pocket for honest Jack, a crust into another for bashful Tom, and a luncheon of cheese was wrapped up with care for the little favorite of his hopeful family. In short, if anything was thrown to the Dog, it was a bone so closely picked that it scarce afforded a pittance to keep life and soul together. "How exactly alike," said the dependant, "is this poor Dog's case and mine! He is watching for a dinner from a master who cannot spare it; I for a place from a needy Lord whose wants, perhaps, are greater than my own, and whose relations are more clamorous than any of this Beggar's brats."

'Tis misery to depend upon patrons whose circumstances make their charity necessary at home.

THE MAN AND THE STONE

Aesop was sent one day by his master Xanthus to see what company were at the public bath. He saw that many who came stumbled, both going in and coming out, over a large Stone that lay at the entrance to the bath, and that only one person had the good sense to remove it. He returned and told his master that there was only one Man at the bath. Xanthus accordingly went, and finding it full of people, demanded of Aesop why he had told him falsely. Aesop replied that only he who had removed the Stone could be considered a Man, and that the rest were not worthy of the name.

A man is judged by his deeds.

THE HARE AND HER MANY FRIENDS

A Hare, who in a civil way complied with everything and everyone, was known as a friend to all the beasts of the forest and plain. While she was out foraging one dawn, she heard the Hunter's horn and the baying of the Hounds. Frantic to escape, she retreated and doubled back, but to no avail. Upon seeing her friend the Horse draw near, she pleaded, "O Horse! Let me ascend to your back that I might be carried safely away from peril." The Horse assured her that, as all her friends were near, she had nothing to worry about, and proceeded on his way. Next she saw the stately Bull, and implored him to transport her out of harm's way. But the Bull told her that he was on his way to court a Cow and, referring her to the Goat some steps behind him, wished her well. When she pleaded with the Goat, he voiced concern that she might find his back uncomfortable and directed her, instead, to the Sheep. "But hounds eat Sheep as well as Hares," said the terrified Sheep before running away. As her last hope, she prostrated herself before the Calf who followed some paces behind the Sheep. "I am but a youngster," said the Calf. "Older and abler passed you by. Should I come to your assistance, those friends might take offense." And so the Calf walked away, leaving the Hare to the mercy of the Hounds.

Imminent peril reveals fair-weather friends.

THE CAMEL

When men first saw the Camel, they were so frightened at his vast size that they fled away. After a time, perceiving the meekness and gentleness of his temper, they summoned courage enough to approach him. Soon afterwards, observing that he was an animal altogether deficient in spirit, they assumed such boldness as to put a bridle in his mouth, and to set a child to drive him.

Use serves to overcome dread.

The Hare and her Many Friends

THE NURSE AND THE WOLF

As a Wolf was hunting up and down for his supper, he passed by the door of a house where a little child was crying loudly. "Hold your tongue," said the Nurse to the child, "or I'll throw you to the Wolf." The Wolf, hearing this, waited near the house, expecting that she would keep her word. The Nurse, however, when the child was quiet, changed her tone, and said, "If the naughty Wolf comes now, we'll beat his brains out for him." The Wolf thought it was then high time to be off. "Serves me right," growled he; "I shall starve to death if I listen to idle threats."

He who threatens most does least.

THE TRAVELERS AND THE CROW

Some Travelers setting out on a journey had not proceeded far when a one-eyed Crow flew across their path. This they took for a bad omen, and it was proposed that they should give up their plan for that day, at least, and turn back again. "What nonsense!" said one of the Travelers, who was of a mocking and merry disposition. "If this Crow could foresee what is to happen to us, he would be equally knowing on his own account; and in that case, do you think he would have been silly enough to go where his eye was to be knocked out of his head?"

Common sense is better than auguries.

THE ANT AND THE COCOON

An Ant, nimbly running about in the sunshine in search of food, came across a Cocoon that was very near its time of change. The Cocoon moved its tail, and thus attracted the attention of the Ant, who then saw for the first time that it was alive. "Poor creature!" cried the Ant

The Nurse and the Wolf

disdainfully; "what a sad fate is yours! While I can run hither and thither, at my pleasure, and, if I wish, ascend the tallest tree, you lie imprisoned here in your shell, with power only to move a joint or two of your scaly tail." The Cocoon heard all this, but did not try to make any reply. A few days after, when the Ant passed that way again, nothing but the shell remained. Wondering what had become of its contents, he felt himself suddenly shaded and fanned by the gorgeous wings of a beautiful Butterfly. "Behold in me," said the Butterfly, "your much-pitied friend! Boast now of your powers to run and climb as long as you can get me to listen." So saying, the Butterfly rose in the air, and, borne along on the summer breeze, was soon lost to the sight of the Ant forever.

Judge not alone by the present.

THE ASS AND THE GRASSHOPPER

An Ass, having heard some Grasshoppers chirping, was highly enchanted; and, desiring to possess the same charms of melody, he demanded what sort of food they lived on to give them such beautiful voices. They replied, "The dew." The Ass resolved that he would live only upon dew, and in a short time died of hunger.

No two people can be treated alike.

JUPITER AND THE MONKEY

Jupiter issued a proclamation to all the Beasts of the forest, and promised a royal reward to the one whose offspring should be deemed the handsomest. The Monkey came with the rest and presented, with all a mother's tenderness, a flat-nosed, hairless, ill-featured young Monkey as a candidate for the promised reward. A general laugh greeted her on the presentation of her son. She resolutely said, "I know not whether Jupiter will allot the prize to my son: but this I do know, that he is at least in the eyes of me, his mother, the dearest, handsomest, and most beautiful of all."

Learn to value your own.

THE TRAVELERS AND THE CHAMELEON

Two Travelers happened on their journey to be engaged in a warm dispute about the Chameleon, which, as you know, changes its color. One of them affirmed it was blue, that he had seen it with his own eyes upon the naked branch of a tree, feeding on the air in a very clear day. The other strongly asserted it was green, and that he had viewed it very closely and minutely upon the broad leaf of a fig tree. Both of them were positive, and the dispute was rising to a quarrel; but a third person luckily coming by, they agreed to refer the question to his decision. "Gentlemen," said the arbitrator, with a smile of great self-satisfaction, "you could not have been more lucky in your reference, as I happen to have caught one of them last night; but, indeed, you are both mistaken, for the creature is totally black." "Black? Impossible!" "Nay," quoth the umpire, with great assurance, "the matter may be soon decided, for I immediately enclosed my Chameleon in a little paper box, and here it is." So saying he drew the box out of his pocket, opened it, and, lo! The Chameleon was as white as snow. The positive disputants looked equally surprised and equally confounded; while the wise reptile, assuming the air of a philosopher, thus admonished them: "Ye children of men, learn moderation in your opinions. 'Tis true, you happen in this present instance to be all in the right, but, pray, for the future allow others to have eyesight as well as yourselves; nor wonder if everyone prefers the testimony of his own senses to those of another."

Have respect for the opinions of others.

THE ASS AND HIS MASTER

A diligent Ass, daily loaded beyond his strength by a severe Master whom he had long served and who fed him very sparingly, happened one day in his old age to be laden with a more than ordinary burden of earthenware. His strength being much impaired, and the road deep and uneven, he unfortunately stumbled, and, unable to recover himself, fell down and broke all the vessels to pieces. His Master, transported with rage, began to beat him unmercifully, against which the poor Ass, lifting up his head as he lay on the ground, thus strongly remonstrated: "Unfeeling wretch! To thine own avaricious cruelty, in first pinching me of food, and then loading me beyond my strength, thou owest the misfortune for which I suffer!"

Lay the blame where it belongs.

THE PLAYFUL ASS

An Ass climbed up to the roof of a building and, frisking about there, broke in the tiling. The owner went up after him, and quickly drove him down, beating him severely with a thick wooden cudgel. The Ass said, "Why, I saw the Monkey do this very thing yesterday, and you all laughed heartily, as if it afforded you very great amusement."

Those who do not know their right place must be taught it.

THE MASTER AND HIS SCHOLAR

As a Schoolmaster was walking upon the bank of a river, not far from his School, he heard a cry, as of someone in distress. Running to the side of the river, he saw one of his Scholars in the water, hanging by the bough of a willow. The boy, it seems, had been learning to swim with corks, and fancying that he could now do without them, had thrown them aside. The force of the stream hurried him out of his depth, and he would certainly have been drowned, had not the

The Ass and his Master

friendly branch of a willow hung in his way. The Master took up the corks, which were lying upon the bank, and threw them to his Scholar. "Let this be a warning to you," said he, "and in your future life never throw away your corks until you are quite sure you have strength and experience enough to swim without them."

Too great assurance is folly.

THE LION AND THE BOAR

On a summer day, when the great heat induced a general thirst, a Lion and a Boar came at the same moment to a small well to drink. They fiercely disputed which of them should drink first, and were soon engaged in the agonies of a mortal combat. On their stopping to take breath for the fiercer renewal of the strife, they saw some Vultures waiting in the distance to feast on the one which should fall first. They at once made up their quarrel, saying, "It is better for us to make friends, than to become the food of Vultures."

The man at strife is always in peril.

THE WILD AND THE TAME GEESE

Two Geese strayed from a farmyard, and swam down a stream to a large swamp, which afforded them an extensive range and plenty of food. A flock of Wild Geese frequently resorted to the same place; and though they were at first so shy as not to suffer the Tame ones to join them, by degrees they became well acquainted and associated freely together. One evening their cackling reached the ears of a Fox that was prowling at no great distance from the swamp. The artful plunderer directed his course through a wood on the borders of it, and was within a few yards of his prey before any of the Geese perceived him. But the alarm was given just as he was springing upon them, and the whole flock instantly ascended into the air, with loud and dissonant cries. "The Fox! The Fox!" the Wild Geese called as they rose swiftly out of his clutches; and they winged their flight into higher regions and were seen no more. "The Fox! The Fox!" replied the two Tame Geese, rising after them; but being heavy, clumsy, and unused to using their wings, they soon dropped down, and became the victims of the Fox.

Those who aspire to a higher station should be able to maintain their position.

THE SORCERESS

Night and silence had now given repose to the whole world when an old, ill-natured Sorceress, in order to exercise her infernal arts, entered into a gloomy wood that trembled at her approach. The scene of her horrid incantations was within the circumference of a large circle, in the center of which was raised an altar, where the hallowed vervain blazed in triangular flames. The mischievous hag pronounced the dreadful words, which bound all hell in obedience to her charms. She blew a raging pestilence from her lips into the neighboring fields; the innocent cattle died, to afford a fit sacrifice to the infernal deities. The moon, by powerful spells drawn down from her orbs, entered the wood; legions of spirits from Pluto's realms appeared before the altar, and demanded her pleasure. "Tell me," said she, "where I shall find what I have lost, my favorite little dog." "How!" cried they all, enraged; "impertinent Beldame! Must the order of nature be inverted, and the repose of every creature disturbed, for the sake of thy little dog?"

There are many people who would unhinge the world to ease themselves of the smallest inconvenience.

THE COCK AND THE HORSES

A Cock once got into a stable, and went about nestling and scratching in the straw among the Horses, who every now and then would stamp and fling out their heels. So the Cock gravely set to work to admonish them. "Pray, my good friends, let us have a care," said he, "that we don't tread on one another."

Disinterested counsel is rare.

THE ENVIOUS GLOW-WORM

A humble Glow-worm lying in a garden was moved with envy on seeing the effect of lights from a brilliant chandelier in a neighboring palace. When, after a short time, the light was seen no more, and the palace was left in total darkness, his wise companion said "Now, you see, we have outlasted those many glaring lights, which, though brighter for a time, yet hasten the more quickly to nothing."

The meteors of fashion rise and fall.

THE LION AND THE ASS

A conceited Ass was once bold enough to bray forth some insulting speeches against the Lion. The Lion at first began to show his teeth, but turning about and seeing who was speaking, merely remarked: "Oh, it is only the Ass! "

Contempt is the best answer for scurrility.

GENIUS, VIRTUE, AND REPUTATION

Genius, Virtue, and Reputation, three great friends, agreed to travel over the island of Great Britain, to see whatever might be worthy of observation. But as some misfortune, said they, may happen to separate us; let us consider before we set out, by what means we may find each other again. "Should it be my ill fate," said Genius, "to be severed from my friends—heaven forbid! You may find me kneeling in devotion before the tomb of Shakespeare; or rapt in some grove where Milton talked with angels; or musing in the grotto where Pope caught inspiration. "Virtue, with a sigh, acknowledged, that her friends were not very numerous; "but were I to lose you," she cried, "with whom I am at present so happily united, I should choose to take sanctuary in the temples of religion, in the palaces of royalty, or in the stately domes of ministers of state; but as it may be my ill fortune to be there denied admittance, inquire for some cottage where contentment has a bower, and there you will certainly find me." "Ah, my dear friends," said Reputation very earnestly, "you, I perceive, when missing, may possibly be recovered; but take care, I entreat you, always to keep sight of me, for if I am once lost, I am never to be retrieved."

There are few things that can be so irreparably lost as reputation.

THE GARDENER AND HIS MASTER

In the midst of a beautiful flower garden there was a large pond filled with carp, tench, perch, and other freshwater fish; it was also intended to water the garden. The foolish Gardener, being particularly careful of the flowers, so emptied the pond of its water that there scarcely remained sufficient to keep the fish alive. His Master, coming down to walk in the garden, and seeing this mismanagement, scolded the Gardener, saying, "Though I am very fond of flowers, I also like to regale myself with fish." The Gardener, being a coarse, ignorant peasant, obeyed his master so precisely that he gave no water to the flowers, in order that the fish might have enough. Some time after the Master again visited his garden, and, to his great mortification, saw his beautiful flowers all dead or drooping. "You blockhead!" he cried; "in the future remember not to use so much water for the flowers as to leave me without fish, nor yet be so liberal to the fish as to kill my beauteous blossoms."

Moderation in everything is best.

THE LYNX AND THE MOLE

Under the covert of a thick wood, at the foot of a tree, as a Lynx lay whetting his teeth and waiting for his prey, he spied a Mole half buried under a hillock of her own raising. "Alas, poor creature," said the Lynx, "how much I pity you! Surely, Jupiter has been very unkind, to debar you from the light of day which rejoices the whole creation. You are certainly not above half alive, and it would be doing you a service to make an end of you." "I thank you for your kindness," replied the Mole, "but I think I have fully as much vivacity as my state and circumstances require. For the rest, I am perfectly well contented with the faculties that Jupiter has given me, who, I am sure, wants not our direction in distributing his gifts. I have not, 'tis true, your piercing eyes, but I have ears which answer all my purposes. Hark! For example, I am warned by a noise which I hear behind you, to flee from danger." So saying, he crept into the earth, while a javelin from the arm of a hunter pierced the quick-sighted Lynx to the heart.

Let none criticize Nature.

THE OWLS, THE BATS, AND THE SUN

The Owls, Bats, and several other Birds of night used to meet together in a thick shade, where they abused their neighbors in a very sociable manner. Their satire at last fell upon the Sun, whom they all agreed to be very troublesome, impertinent, and inquisitive. The Sun chanced to overhear his critics, but contented himself with replying: "Ladies, I care little for your opinion, but I wonder how you dare abuse one who could in an instant destroy you; however, the only answer I shall give you or the revenge I shall take of you, is to shine on."

Gossips are best answered by silence.

THE RIVERS AND THE SEA

The Rivers joined together to complain to the Sea, saying, "Why is it that when we flow into your tides so potable and sweet, you work in us such a change, and make us salty and unfit to drink?" The Sea, perceiving that they intended to throw the blame on him, said, "Pray, cease to flow into me, and then you will not be made briny."

Some find fault with those things by which they are chiefly benefited.

THE WOLF IN DISGUISE

A Wolf, who by his frequent visits to a flock of sheep in his neighborhood began to be extremely well known to them, thought it expedient, for the more successfully carrying on of his depredations, to appear in a new character. To this end he disguised himself in a shepherd's habit; and resting his forefeet upon a stick, which served him by way of crook, he softly made his approach toward the fold. It happened that the shepherd and his dog were both of them extended on the grass, fast asleep, so that he would certainly have succeeded in his project, if he had not imprudently attempted to imitate the shepherd's voice. The horrid noise awakened them both; when the Wolf, encumbered with his disguise, and finding it impossible either to resist or to flee, yielded up his life an easy prey to the shepherd's dog.

Hypocrites frequently lay themselves open to discovery by overacting their parts.

THE MAN AND HIS DOGS

A certain Man, detained by a storm in his country house, first killed all of his Sheep, and then his Goats, for the maintenance of his household. The storm still continuing, he was obliged to slaughter his yoke Oxen for food. On seeing this, his Dogs took counsel together, and

The Wolf in Disguise

said, "It is time for us to be off: for if the Master spare not his Oxen, who work for his gain, how can we expect him to spare us?"

He is not to be trusted as a friend who ill-treats those on whom he depends.

THE LOBSTERS

It chanced on a time that the shell of a boiled Lobster was thrown on the seashore, where it was quickly espied by one of the same tribe, who, young, ignorant, and vain, viewed it with admiration and delight. "See," said she, addressing her mother, who was at her side; "behold the beauty of one of our family, thus decked out in noble scarlet, so rich in color that no coral can surpass it in brilliancy! I shall have no rest till I am equally as fine, and have ceased to see myself the dingy object I am at present." "Vain creature!" replied the mother; "know that this same tawdry finery which you so earnestly covet was only acquired by death. And learn from this terrible example to be humble and content, obscure and safe."

Fine feathers are a sign neither of wealth nor of happiness.

THE TWO SCYTHES

It so happened that a couple of mower's Scythes were placed together in the same barn: one of them was without its proper handle, and therefore remained useless and rusty; the other was complete, bright, and in good order, and was frequently made use of in the hands of the mowers. "My good neighbor," said the rusty one, "I much pity you, who labor so much for the good of others, and withal so constantly are fretted with that odious whetstone, that scours you till you strike fire, while I repose in perfect ease and quiet." "Give me leave," replied the bright one, "to explain to you, neighbor, the difference of our conditions. I must own that I labor, but then I am well rewarded by the consideration that it is for the benefit of multitudes, and this gives me all my importance; it is true, also, that I am sharpened by a harsh whetstone, but this still increases my usefulness, while you remain the insignificant and helpless victim of your pride and idleness, and in the end fall prey to a devouring rust, useless, unpitied, and unknown."

Idleness is attended by misery unknown to the industrious.

THE LION AND THE HARE

A Lion came across a Hare, who lay fast asleep. He was just in the act of seizing her when a fine young Hart trotted by, and he left the Hare to follow him. The Hare, scared by the noise, awoke, and scudded away. The Lion was not able after a long chase to catch the Hart, and returned to feed upon the Hare. On finding that the Hare also had run off, he said, "I am rightly served for having let go the food I had in my hand for the chance of obtaining more."

Be content with an assured income.

THE SPANISH CAVALIER

One day a quarrel about a lady happened between a Spanish Cavalier and a Dutchman. "Satisfaction" was the word, and they met to decide the dispute. The contest was fierce and bloody, for they closed at the first encounter; and the Don, being mortally wounded, fell down, and cried out to an intimate friend of his who was running to his assistance, but too late, "My good friend, for the love of Heaven, be so good as to bury me before anybody strips me!" Having said this, so great a quantity of blood flowed from his wound that he died immediately. Now this odd request of the Spaniard to his friend raised everybody's curiosity (as it generally happens in things prohibited) to see him divested of his clothing, especially since it was the dying request and entreaty of a worthy hero of that wise nation who never speak at random, nor drop a word that is not full of mysteries, and each mystery full of sense, so that everyone had a great desire to know the meaning of it; and, in spite of all his friend could do to prevent it, he was stripped immediately. Upon search, this spruce blade, who was completely dressed a la Cavalier, and with a curious ruff about his neck worth more than all the rest of his finery, was found to have never a shirt to his back: at which the spectators could not help smiling, although the event was so pitiable.

The vain prefer honor to life.

THE OAK AND THE WILLOW

A conceited Willow had once the vanity to challenge his mighty neighbor the Oak to a trial of strength. It was to be determined by the next storm, and Æolus was addressed by both parties, to exert his most powerful efforts. This was no sooner asked than granted; and a violent hurricane arose. The pliant Willow, bending from the blast, or shrinking under it, evaded all its force; while the generous Oak, disdaining to give way, opposed its fury, and was torn up by the roots. Immediately the Willow began to exult, and to claim the victory; when thus the fallen Oak interrupted his exultation: "Callest thou this a trial of strength? Poor wretch! Not to thy strength, but weakness; not to thy boldly facing danger, but meanly skulking from it, thou owest thy present safety. I am an oak, though fallen; thou still a willow, though unhurt; but who, except so mean a wretch as thyself, would prefer an ignominious life, preserved by craft or cowardice, to the glory of meeting death in a brave contention?"

The courage of meeting death in an honorable cause is more commendable than any address or artifice we can use to evade it.

THE LION AND THE SNAKE

A loudly Lion, who was seeking for his prey, by chance saw a Snake basking in the sun, when, being rather sharp-set by hunger, and disappointed in his object, he, with a haughty air, spurned the reptile with his paw, as not being agreeable to his stomach. But the enraged Snake turned on him, gave him a mortal sting, and said: "Die, imperious tyrant! And let thy example show that no power can always save a despot, and that even reptiles have rights."

The tyrant lays himself open to attack.

THE LION AND THE EAGLE

An Eagle stayed his flight, and entreated a Lion to make an alliance with him to their mutual advantage. The Lion replied, "I have no objection, but you must excuse me for requiring you to find surety for your good faith; for how can I trust anyone as a friend, who is able to fly away from his bargain whenever he pleases?"

Try before you trust.

THE SILKWORM AND THE SPIDER

A Silkworm was one day working at her shroud: the Spider, her neighbor, weaving her web with the greatest swiftness, looked down with contempt on the slow, although beautiful, labors of the Silkworm. "What do you think of my web, my lady?" she cried; "see how large it is! I began it only this morning, and here it is half finished. Look and acknowledge that I work much quicker than you." "Yes," said the Silkworm, "but your webs, which are at first designed only as base traps to ensnare the harmless, are destroyed as soon as they are seen, and swept away as dirt and worse than useless; while mine are preserved with the greatest care, and in time become ornaments for princes." So saying, my Lady Silkworm took up her thread again, and continued to weave her beautiful fabric with even greater care.

Not how much, but how well.

THE ASTRONOMER[9]

An Astronomer used to go out at night to observe the stars. One evening, as he wandered through the suburbs with his whole attention fixed on the sky, he fell unawares into a ditch. While he lamented and bewailed his sores and bruises, and cried loudly for help, a neighbor ran to the ditch and learning what had happened said: "Hark ye, old fellow, why, in striving to pry into what is in Heaven, do you not manage to see what is on earth?"

Do not overlook the ordinary for the wondrous.

THE GOOSE AND THE SWANS

A vain and empty Goose one day complained shrilly to members of her flock of the ill regard given geese compared to other birds. "See the Peacock, yonder," she gestured with a flap of her wing, "and how she hides her flaws behind her gaudy feathers. Were she and I stripped, I pledge my word that all would find me the finer bird." Crossing the mead to where a bunch of Swans sported in the stream, she continued her tirade. "Again, what arrogance we see," she cackled, indicating the Swans. "Because we Geese are known to skim the waters delicately, these base creatures think to mimic us with their awkward and noisy splashing." So saying, she plunged into the water and, spreading her plumes, tried to assume the Swan's stately crest. "Conceited thing, elate with pride," complained one of Swans. "Though you put on airs, your oafishness reveals you to be just a silly Goose."

Foppery is the pride of fools.

THE DOG AND THE OYSTER

A Dog used to eating eggs saw an Oyster and, opening his mouth to its widest extent, swallowed it down with the utmost relish, supposing it to be an egg. Soon afterwards suffering great pain in his stomach, he said, "I deserve all this torment, for my folly in thinking that everything round must be an egg."

They who act without sufficient thought will often fall into unsuspected danger.

THE CORMORANT AND THE FISHES

A Cormorant, whose eyes were so dim with age that he could not discern his prey at the bottom of the waters, devised a trick to supply his wants. "Hark you, friend," said he to a Gudgeon, whom he found swimming near the surface of a certain canal, "if you have any regard for yourself or your brethren, go at once and tell them from me that the owner of this piece of water means to drag it a week hence." The Gudgeon immediately swam away and made his report of this terrible news to a general assembly of the Fishes, who unanimously agreed to send him back as their ambassador to the Cormorant. He was to return their thanks for the intelligence, and to add their entreaties that, as he had been so good as to inform them of their danger, he would be graciously pleased to put them into the way of escaping it. "That I will, most readily," replied the artful Cormorant, "and assist you with my best services into the bargain. You have only to collect yourselves together at the top of the water, and I will undertake to transport you, one by one, to my own residence, at the side of a solitary pool, to which no creature but myself ever found the way." The project was approved by the unwary Fishes, and quickly performed by the deceitful Cormorant. When he had placed them in a shallow piece of water, the bottom of which his eyes could easily discern, they were all devoured by him in their turn, as his hunger or luxury required.

It is not wise to trust an enemy or stranger so far as to put yourself in his power.

The Cormorant and the Fishes

THE BLIND SHEEP

A certain poor Sheep was so unfortunate as some years before his death to become blind, when the Owl, who had assumed to himself the profession of Oculist to his Majesty the Eagle, undertook to cure him. On the morning when the operation was to have been performed, the Sheep placed himself in the seat, and asked the Oculist if all things were ready for cure. The Oculist answered, "Yes. My instruments and plasters are all prepared, and nothing is wanting." "Ay," said the Sheep, " the things you have mentioned are of least importance toward giving one that satisfaction I desire by the recovery of my sight. Tell me, how goes the world?" "Why, even just as it did," says the Owl, "when you fell blind." "Sayest thou so, friend?" replied the Sheep. "Then, prithee, hold thy hand and proceed no farther, for I would not give a blade of grass to recover my sight if I must again be punished in beholding enormities so odious in the eyes of all innocent creatures on earth."

No remedy for the world's ills is as great an ill as any.

THE LION, THE BEAR, THE MONKEY, AND THE FOX

The tyrant of the forest issued a proclamation, commanding all his subjects to repair immediately to his royal den. Among the rest, the Bear made his appearance; but pretending to be offended with the steams that issued from the monarch's apartments, he was imprudent enough to hold his nose in his majesty's presence. This insolence was so highly resented, that the Lion in a rage laid him dead at his feet. The Monkey, observing what had passed, trembled for his carcass, and attempted to conciliate favor by the most abject flattery. He began with protesting, that for his part, he thought the apartments were perfumed with Arabian spices, and exclaiming against the rudeness of the Bear, admired the beauty of his majesty's paws, so happily formed, he said, to correct the insolence of clowns. This fulsome adulation, instead of being received as he expected, proved no less offensive than the rudeness of the Bear, and the courtly Monkey was in like manner extended

The Lion, the Bear, the Monkey, and the Fox

by the side of Sir Bruin. And now his majesty cast his eye upon the Fox. "Well, Fox," said he, "and what scent do you discover here?" "Great prince," replied the cautious Fox, "my nose was never esteemed my most distinguishing sense, and at present I would by no means venture to give my opinion, as I have unfortunately got a terrible cold."

It is often more prudent to suppress our sentiments than either to flatter, or to rail.

THE MASTIFF AND THE GOOSE

A Goose, once upon a time, took up her abode by a pond, which she immediately laid claim to. If any other animal, without the least design to offend, happened to pass that way, the Goose immediately flew at it. The pond, she said, was hers, and she would maintain her right to it, and support her honor while she had a bill to hiss, or a wing to flutter. In this manner she drove away Ducks, Pigs, Chickens, nay, even the insidious Cat was seen to scamper. A Mastiff, however, happened to pass by, and thought it no harm if he should lap a little of the water, as he was thirsty. "Get away!" hissed our valiant Keeper of the pond, as soon as she saw him approaching. "Get away I tell you! It's mine!" and she flew at him like a Fury, pecked at him with her beak, and slapped him with her feathers. The Mastiff grew angry, and had twenty times a mind to give her a sly snap, but controlled his wrath, because his master was nigh. "You fool!" cried he. "Those who have neither strength nor weapons to fight should at least be civil." So saying, he quenched his thirst in spite of the Goose, and followed his master.

Arrogance inspires contempt.

THE CROW AND THE RAVEN

A Crow was very jealous of the Raven, because he was considered a bird of good omen, and always attracted the attention of men, as indicating by his flight the good or evil course of future events. Seeing some travelers approaching, she flew up into a tree, and perching herself on one of the branches, cawed as loudly as she could. The travelers turned towards the sound, and wondered what it boded, when one of them said to his companion, "Let us proceed on our journey, my friend, for it is only the caw of a Crow, and her cry, you know, is no omen."

Those who assume a character that does not belong to them only make themselves ridiculous.

THE FROG AND THE HEN

"Dear me!" said the Frog to himself one day as he heard a Hen cackling near his bog; "what a very noisy creature that Hen is to be sure! Mrs. Hen," he called out, "do be quiet; you'll alarm the whole neighborhood. Really, one would think you had made a grand discovery. What is the cause or the meaning of all this uproar?" "My dear sir, have patience with me; I've laid an egg." "Upon my word you make a great fuss over one egg." "Well, well, I am sorry to see you so ill-tempered at my little song of joy, when I've endured without a murmur your croaking all day and night long. But I claim to have done some good, though that may be small. You, on the contrary, should hold your tongue, for you certainly do no good whatever."

Talkers seldom become doers.

THE ASS AND THE FROGS

An Ass, carrying a load of wood, passed through a pond. As he was crossing through the water he lost his footing, and stumbled and fell, and not being able to rise on account of his load, he groaned heavily. Some Frogs frequenting the pool heard his lamentation, and said,

"What would you do if you had to live here always as we do, when you make such a fuss about a mere fall into the water?"

Men often bear little grievances with less courage than they do large misfortunes.

THE TWO LIZARDS

Two Lizards were basking under a wall. "How contemptible is our condition!" said one of them. "We exist, 'tis true, but that is all; for we hold no sort of rank in the creation, and are utterly unnoticed by the world. Cursed obscurity! Why was I not rather born a Stag to range at large, the pride and glory of some royal forest?" Just then a pack of hounds was heard in full cry after the very creature he was envying who, being quite spent with the chase, was torn to pieces by the dogs in sight of the two Lizards. "And this is the lordly Stag whose place you wish to hold?" said the wiser Lizard to his complaining friend. "Let his sad fate teach you to be content with your lot."

Contentment is not a matter of rank or position.

THE LION AND THE BULL

A Lion, greatly desirous to capture a Bull and yet afraid to attack him on account of his great size, resorted to a trick to ensure his destruction. He approached him and said, "I have slain a fine Sheep, my friend; and if you will come home and partake of him with me, I shall be delighted to have your company." The Lion said this in the hope that, as the Bull was in the act of reclining to eat, he might attack him to advantage, and make his meal on him. The Bull, however, on his approach to the den, saw the huge spits and giant caldrons, and no sign whatever of the Sheep, and, without saying a word, quietly took his departure. The Lion inquired why he went off so abruptly without a word of salutation to his host, who had not given him any cause of

The Two Lizards

offense. "I have reasons enough," said the Bull. "I see no indication whatever of your having slaughtered a Sheep, while I do see, very plainly, every preparation for your dining on a Bull."

Forewarned is forearmed.

THE TWO RATS

A cunning old Rat discovered in his rounds a most tempting piece of cheese, which was placed in a trap. But being well aware that if he touched it he would be caught, he slyly sought one of his young friends, and, under the mask of friendship, informed him of the prize. "I cannot use it myself," said he, "for I have just made a hearty meal." The inexperienced youngster thanked him with gratitude for the news, and heedlessly sprang upon the tempting bait; on which the trap closed and instantly destroyed him. His companion, being now quite secure, quietly ate up the cheese.

Do not listen to every passerby.

THE TWO SPRINGS

Two Springs which issued from the same mountain began their course together; one of them took her way in a silent and gentle stream, while the other rushed along with a sounding and rapid current. "Sister," said the latter, "at the rate you move, you will probably be dried up before you advance much farther; whereas, for myself, I will venture a wager, that within two or three hundred furlongs I shall become navigable, and after distributing commerce and wealth wherever I flow, I shall majestically proceed to pay my tribute to the ocean: so farewell, dear sister, and patiently submit to your fate." Her sister made no reply, but calmly descending to the meadows below, increased her stream by numberless little rills, which she collected in her progress, till at length she was enabled to rise into a considerable river; while the proud stream, which had the vanity to depend solely upon her own sufficiency, continued a shallow brook, and was glad at last to be helped forward, by throwing herself into the arms of her despised sister.

There is more to be expected from sedate and silent, than from noisy, turbulent, and ostentatious beginnings.

THE HUNGRY CAT AND THE PIGEONS

A certain man brought up a Cat, which he fed but sparingly, and the poor animal, being very ravenous and not contented with her ordinary food, was wont to hunt about in every corner for more. One day, passing by a dovecote, she saw some young Pigeons that were scarcely fledged, and her mouth watered for a taste of them. To gratify her taste at once she climbed up into the dovecote, never caring to find out whether the master was in the way or not. But no sooner did the owner of the birds see the Cat enter than he shut the doors and stopped up all the holes where she might get out again; and having caught the thieving Puss red-handed he hanged her up at the corner of the pigeon-house. Soon after the Cat's master passed that way, and seeing his Cat, exclaimed, "Unfortunate creature, hadst thou been contented with thy meaner food, thou hadst not now been in this condition!"

The insatiable are the procurers of their own untimely ends.

THE TROOPER AND HIS HORSE

As a Trooper was currying his Horse, he noticed that one of the shoe-nails had dropped out, yet he postponed for the present striking in another nail. Soon after he was summoned by sound of trumpet to join his corps, which was commanded to advance rapidly and charge the enemy. In the heat of the action the loose shoe fell off, his horse

The Trooper and his Horse

became lame, stumbled, and threw his rider to the ground. The Trooper was immediately slain by the enemy.

Small duties neglected become great perils.

THE LAMB AND THE WOLF

A flock of Sheep were feeding in a meadow while their Dogs were asleep and their Shepherd at a distance, playing on his pipe beneath the shade of a spreading elm. A young, inexperienced Lamb, observing a half-starved Wolf peering through the pales of the enclosure, entered into conversation with him. "Pray, what are you seeking for here?" said the Lamb. "I am looking," replied the Wolf, "for some tender grass; for nothing, you know, is more pleasant than to feed in a fresh pasture, and to slake one's thirst at a crystal stream, both of which I perceive you enjoy here. Happy creature," continued he, "how much I envy your lot, who are in full possession of the utmost I desire; for philosophy has long taught me to be satisfied with a little!" "It seems, then," returned the Lamb, "that those who say you feed on flesh accuse you falsely, since a little grass will easily content you. If this be true, let us for the future live like brethren, and feed together." So saying, the simple Lamb crept through the fence, and at once became a prey to the pretended philosopher, and a sacrifice to his own inexperience and credulity.

Experience is a dear school, but fools will learn in no other.

THE MASTIFF AND THE CURS

A stout and honest Mastiff that guarded the village where he lived against robbers was one day walking with one of his Puppies by his side when all the little Dogs in the street gathered about him and barked at him. The Puppy was so enraged at this insult that he asked his father why he did not fall upon them and tear them to pieces. To which the Mastiff answered, with great composure of mind, "If there were no Curs, I should be no Mastiff."

Nobility is its own defense.

THE ASS AND HIS DRIVER

An Ass being driven along the high road suddenly started off and bolted to the brink of a deep precipice. When he was in the act of throwing himself over, his owner, seizing him by the tail, endeavored to pull him back. The Ass, persisting in his effort, the Man let him go and said, "Conquer: but conquer to your cost."

Fools persist in their own way even though it leads them to grief.

THE MICE AND THE TRAP

Once upon a time some Mice saw a bit of toasted bacon hanging up in a very little room, the door of which, being open, enticed them to fall to work on the dainty morsel with greedy appetites. But two or three of them took particular notice that there was but one way into the room, and, therefore, but one way to get out of it; so that if the door by misfortune or art should chance to be shut, they would all inevitably be taken. They could not, therefore, bring themselves to enter, but said that they would rather content themselves with homely fare in plenty, than for the sake of a dainty bit run the risk of being taken and lost forever. The other Mice, however, declared that they saw no danger, and ran into the room and began to eat the bacon with great delight. But they soon heard the door fall down, and saw that they were all taken. Then the fear of approaching death so seized them that they found no relish for the delicious food, but stood shivering and fasting until the Cook who had set the Trap came and put an end to them. The wise Mice, who had contented themselves with their usual food, fled into their holes, and by that means preserved their lives.

He who embarks upon an enterprise should be able to see his way out of it.

THE LION AND THE FOX

A Fox entered into partnership with a Lion on the pretence of becoming his servant. Each undertook his proper duty in accordance with his own nature and powers. The Fox discovered and pointed out the prey, the Lion sprang on it, and seized it. The Fox soon became jealous of the Lion carrying off the Lion's share, and said that he would no longer find out the prey, but would capture it on his own account. The next day he attempted to snatch a lamb from the fold, but fell himself a prey to the huntsmen and hounds.

Do not trust too greatly to your prowess.

THE ROPE DANCE

A Boy whose stock of patience was none of the largest went to take lessons in dancing on the tightrope of an old and experienced teacher. The lad often objected to the use of the balancing-pole, and one day exclaimed to his master, "Why, sir, what is the good of this great long pole? I could get on much better without it. It is always in my way, and is heavy besides. I am strong and active, and am quite sure that I could dance better without this or any other pole. Now just watch my steps, and judge for yourself"; saying which, the youngster threw the pole to the ground, and in half a minute he lay beside it, having lost his hold of the rope almost as soon as he threw aside the pole. "Ah, you silly, self-willed boy!" exclaimed the master; "you would have your own way, and so you have nearly broken your neck."

Baseless overconfidence must yield to art, advice, and method.

MINERVA AND THE OWL

"My most solemn and wise bird," said Minerva one day to her Owl, "having hitherto admired you for your profound taciturnity, I have now a mind for variety to have you display your parts in discourse; for silence is only admirable in one who can, when he pleases, triumph by his eloquence and charm with graceful conversation." The Owl replied by solemn grimaces, and made dumb signs. Minerva bid him lay aside that affectation and begin; but he only shook his wise head and remained silent. Whereupon Minerva, provoked with this mimicry of wisdom, commanded him to speak immediately, on pain of her displeasure. The Owl, seeing no remedy, drew up close to Minerva, and whispered very softly in her ear this sage remark: "Since the world has grown so depraved, they ought to be esteemed most wise who have eyes to see and wit to hold their tongues."

Silence sometimes speaks louder than words.

THE BEE AND THE SPIDER

The Bee and the Spider once entered into a warm debate which was the better artist. The Spider urged her skill in the mathematics, and asserted that no one was half so well acquainted as herself with the construction of lines, angles, squares, and circles; that the web she daily wove was a specimen of art inimitable by any other creature in the universe; and besides, that her works were derived from herself alone, the product of her own bowels; whereas the boasted honey of the Bee was stolen from every herb and flower of the field; nay, that she had obligations even to the meanest weeds. To this the Bee replied that she was in hopes that the art of extracting honey from the meanest weeds would at least have been allowed her as an excellence; and that as to her stealing sweets from the herbs and flowers of the field, her skill was there so conspicuous, that no flower ever suffered the least diminution of its fragrance from so delicate an operation. Then, as to the Spider's vaunted knowledge in the construction of lines and angles, she believed she might safely rest the merits of her cause on the regularity alone of her combs; but since she could add to this the sweetness and excellence of her honey, and the various purposes for which her wax was employed, she had nothing to fear from a comparison of her skill with that of the weaver of a flimsy cobweb; for the value of every art, she observed, is chiefly to be estimated by its use.

Neither ingenuity nor learning is entitled to regard but in proportion as they contribute to the happiness of life.

THE APE AND THE CARPENTER

An Ape sat looking at a Carpenter who was cleaving a piece of wood with two wedges, which he put into the cleft one after another as the split opened. The Carpenter leaving his work half done, the Ape must needs try his hand at log-splitting, and coming to the piece of wood, pulled out the wedge that was in it without knocking in the other. The wood closing again held the poor Monkey by his fore paws so fast that he was not able to get away. The surly Carpenter, when he returned, knocked the prisoner's brains out for meddling with his work.

It is easier to get into mischief than to get out again.

THE PLAGUE AMONG THE BEASTS

A mortal distemper once raged among the Beasts, and swept away prodigious numbers. After it had continued some time without abatement, the Beasts decided that it was a judgment inflicted upon them for their sins, and a day was appointed for a general confession; when it was agreed that he who appeared to be the greatest sinner should suffer death as an atonement for the rest. The Fox was appointed father confessor upon the occasion; and the Lion, with great generosity, condescended to be the first in making public confession. "For my

The Ape and the Carpenter

part," said he, "I must acknowledge I have been an enormous offender. I have killed many innocent Sheep in my time; nay, once, but it was a case of necessity, I made a meal of the Shepherd." The Fox, with much gravity, owned that these in any other but the king, would have been inexpiable crimes; but that His Majesty had certainly a right to a few silly Sheep; nay, and to the Shepherd, too, in case of necessity. The judgment of the Fox was applauded by all the larger animals; and the Tiger, the Leopard, the Bear, and the Wolf made confession of many sins of the like nature; which were all excused with the same lenity and mercy, and their crimes accounted so venial as scarce to deserve the name of offenses. At last, a poor penitent Ass, with great contrition, acknowledged that once going through the churchyard, being very hungry and tempted by the sweetness of the grass, he had cropped a little of it, not more, however, in quantity than the tip of his tongue; he was very sorry for the misdemeanor, and hoped—"Hope!" exclaimed the Fox, with singular zeal; "what canst thou hope for after the commission of so heinous a crime? What! Eat the churchyard grass! Oh, sacrilege! This, this is the flagrant wickedness, my brethren, which has drawn the wrath of Heaven upon our heads, and this the notorious offender whose death must make atonement for all our transgressions." So saying, he ordered his entrails for sacrifice, and the Beasts went to dinner upon the rest of his carcass.

It is easy to find fault with the helpless.

THE LION AND THE SLAVE

A runaway Slave once met up with a Lion who had trod upon a thorn, and who came up towards him wagging his tail, and holding up his lame foot, as if he would say, "I am a suppliant, and seek your aid." The Slave boldly examined the wound, discovered the thorn, and placing the Lion's foot upon his lap, pulled it out and relieved the animal of his pain. The Lion joyfully returned to the forest. Some time after, the Slave was captured and was condemned to be cast to the Lion. The Lion proved to be the one he had befriended. On being released from his cage, he recognized the Slave as the man who had healed him, and, instead of attacking him, approached and placed his foot upon the man's lap. The King, as soon as he had heard the tale, ordered the Lion to be set free again in the forest, and the Slave to be pardoned and given his liberty.

One good deed deserves another.

THE PARROT

A certain Widower, in order to amuse his solitary hours, and in some measure supply the conversation of his departed helpmate of loquacious memory, determined to purchase a Parrot. With this view he applied to a dealer in birds, who showed him a large collection of parrots of various kinds. While they were exercising their talkative talents before him, one repeating the cries of the town, another asking for a cup of sack, and a third bawling out for a coach, he observed a green Parrot perched in a thoughtful manner at a distance upon the foot of a table. "And so you, my grave gentleman," said he, "are quite silent." To which the Parrot replied, like a philosophical bird, "I think the more." Pleased with this sensible answer, our Widower immediately paid down his price, and took home the bird; conceiving great things from a creature who had given so striking a specimen of his parts. But after having instructed him during a whole month, he found to his great disappointment that he could get nothing more from him than the fatiguing repetition of the same dull sentence, "I think the more." "I find," said he in great wrath, "that thou art a most invincible fool, and ten times more a fool was I for having formed a favorable opinion of thy abilities upon no better foundation than an affected solemnity."

Gravity, though sometimes the mien of wisdom, is often found to be the mask of ignorance.

THE ROSE AND THE AMARANTH

An Amaranth, planted in a garden near a Rosebush, thus addressed it: "What a lovely flower is the Rose, a favorite alike with gods and with men. I envy you your beauty and your perfume." The Rose replied, "I indeed, dear Amaranth, flourish but for a brief season! If no cruel hand pluck me from my stem, yet I must perish by an early doom. But you are immortal, and never fade, but bloom forever in renewed youth."

Lasting things are best.

THE SNAIL AND THE STATUE

A Statue of the Medicean Venus was erected in a grove sacred to beauty and the fine arts. Its modest attitude, its elegant proportions, assisted by the situation in which it was placed, attracted the regard of every delicate observer. A Snail, who had fixed himself beneath the moulding of the pedestal, beheld with an evil eye the admiration it excited. Wherefore, watching his opportunity, he strove, by trailing his filthy slime over every limb and feature, to obliterate those beauties that he could not endure to hear so much applauded. An honest linnet, however, who observed him at his dirty work, took the freedom to assure him that he would infallibly lose his labor: For although, said he, to an injudicious eye, thou mayst sully the perfections of this finished piece; yet a more accurate and close inspector will admire its beauty, through all the blemishes with which thou hast endeavored to disguise it.

It is the fate of envy to attack even those characters which are superior to its malice.

THE CROW AND THE SHEEP

A troublesome Crow seated herself on the back of a Sheep. The Sheep, much against his will, carried her backward and forward for a long time, and at last said, "If you had treated a Dog in this way, you would have had your deserts from his sharp teeth." To this the Crow replied, "I despise the weak, and yield to the strong. I know whom I may bully, and whom I must flatter; and I thus prolong my life to a good old age."

The contemptible will ever be imposed upon.

THE BOY AND THE FILBERTS

A Boy once thrust his hand into a pitcher that was full of figs and filberts. He grasped as many as his fist could possibly hold, but when he tried to draw it out, the narrowness of the neck prevented him. Not liking to lose any of them, but unable to draw out his hand full, he burst into tears and bitterly bemoaned his hard fortune. An honest fellow who stood by gave him this wise and reasonable advice: "Grasp only half the quantity, my boy, and you will easily succeed."

Do not seize more than you can carry away.

THE TRAVELERS AND THE PLANE TREE

Two Travelers, worn out by the heat of the summer's sun, laid themselves down at noon under the wide-spreading branches of a Plane tree. As they rested under its shade, one of the Travelers said to the other, "What a singularly useless tree is the Plane! It bears no fruit, and is not of the least service to man." The Plane tree, interrupting him, said, "You ungrateful fellow! Do you, while receiving benefits from me, and resting under my shade, dare to describe me as useless and unprofitable?"

Some men despise their best blessings.

THE THRUSH AND THE FOWLER[10]

A Thrush was feeding on a myrtle tree, and did not move from it, on account of the deliciousness of its berries. A Fowler observing her staying so long in one spot, having well birdlimed his reeds, caught her. The Thrush, being at the point of death, exclaimed, "O foolish creature that I am! For the sake of a little pleasant food I have deprived myself of my life."

Do not lose sight of the future in the present.

THE OSTRICH AND THE PELICAN

The Ostrich one day met the Pelican and observed her breast all bloody. "Good God!" he said to her, "what is the matter? What accident has befallen you? You certainly have been seized by some savage beast of prey, and have with difficulty escaped from his merciless claws." "Do not be surprised, friend," replied the Pelican; "no such accident, nor indeed anything more than common, hath happened to me. I have only been engaged in my ordinary employment of tending my nest, of feeding my dear little ones, and nourishing them with the vital blood from my bosom." "Your answer," returned the Ostrich, "astonishes me still more than the horrid figure you make. What, is this your practice, to tear your own flesh, to spill your own blood, and to sacrifice yourself in this cruel manner to the importunate cravings of your young ones? I know not which to pity most, your misery or your folly. Be advised by me: have some regard for yourself, and leave off this barbarous custom of mangling your own body; as for your children, commit them to the care of Providence, and make yourself quite easy about them. My example may be of use to you. I lay my eggs upon the ground, and just cover them lightly over with sand; if they have the good luck to escape being crushed by the tread of man or beast, the warmth of the sun broods upon, and hatches them, and in due time my young ones come forth; I leave them to be nursed by nature, and fostered by the elements; I give myself no trouble about them, and I neither know nor care what becomes of them." "Unhappy wretch," says the Pelican, "who hardenest thyself against thy own offspring, and through want of natural affection renderest thy travail fruitless to thyself! Who knowest not the sweets of a parent's anxiety; the tender delights of a mother's sufferings! It is not I, but thou, that art cruel to thy own flesh. Thy insensibility may exempt thee from a temporary inconvenience, and an inconsiderable pain, but at the same time it makes thee inattentive to a most necessary duty, and incapable of relishing the pleasure that attends it; a pleasure, the most exquisite that nature hath indulged to us; in which pain itself is swallowed up and lost, or only serves to heighten the enjoyment."

The pleasures of parental fondness make large amends for all its anxieties.

THE TWO SOLDIERS AND THE ROBBER

Two Soldiers traveling together were set upon by a Robber. The one fled away; the other stood his ground, and defended himself with his stout right hand. The Robber being slain, the timid companion ran up and drew his sword, and said: "I'll at him and I'll take care he shall learn whom he has attacked." On this he who had fought with the Robber made answer, "I only wish that you had helped me just now, even if it had been only with those words, for I should have been the more encouraged, believing them to be true; but now put up your sword in its sheath and hold your equally useless tongue, till you can deceive others who do not know you."

A coward is soon found out.

THE PHILOSOPHER AMONG THE TOMBS

A sage Philosopher, well versed in all knowledge natural as well as moral, was one day found in a cemetery deeply absorbed in contemplating two human skeletons which lay before him—the one that of a duke, the other that of a common beggar. After some time he made this exclamation: "If skillful anatomists have made it appear that the bones, nerves, muscles, and entrails of all men are made after the same manner and form, surely this is a most convincing proof that true nobility is situated in the mind, and not in the blood."

In death, the rich and the poor meet together.

THE ELEPHANT AND THE ASSEMBLY OF ANIMALS

The wise Elephant, whose efforts were always directed towards the benefit of his society, saw with much concern the many abuses among the Beasts, which called loudly for reform. He therefore assembled them, and, with all due respect and humility, began a long sermon, wherein he spoke plainly to them about their vices and bad habits. He called their attention especially to their idle ways; their greed, cruelty, envy, hatred, treachery, and deceit. To many of his auditors this speech was excellent and they listened with open-mouthed attention, especially such as the innocent Dove, the faithful Dog, the obedient Camel, the harmless Sheep, and the industrious Ant; the busy Bee also approved much of this lecture. Another part of the audience were extremely offended, and could scarcely endure so long an oration; the Tiger, for instance, and the Wolf were exceedingly tired, and the Serpent hissed with all his might, while a murmur of disapprobation burst from the Wasp, the Drone, the Hornet, and the Fly. The Grasshopper hopped disdainfully away from the assembly, the Sloth was indignant, and the insolent Ape mimicked the orator. The Elephant, seeing the tumult, concluded his discourse with these words: "My advice is addressed equally to all, but remember that those who feel hurt by any remarks of mine acknowledge their guilt. The innocent are unmoved."

It is the bit dog that howls.

The Elephant and the Assembly of Animals

THE FLEA AND THE MAN

A Man very much annoyed by a Flea caught him at last and said, "Who are you who dare to feed on my limbs, and to cost me so much trouble in catching you?" The Flea replied, "O my dear sir, pray spare my life, and destroy me not, for I cannot possibly do you much harm." The Man, laughing, replied, "Now you shall certainly die by mine own hands, for no evil, whether it be small or large, ought to be tolerated."

Small evils are as bad as large ones.

TWO THIEVES AND THE BEAR

A couple of Thieves, knowing of a Calf that was kept in an Ox's stall, had determined to steal it away in the dark, and accordingly appointed the hour of midnight for meeting at the place. One of them was to keep watch on the outside, while the other was to go into the stall and lift the Calf out of the window. On the night proposed, they accordingly went to the place, and one of them entered the window of the Ox's stall, while he that remained on watch, not without much fear of detection, desired his companion to make as much haste as possible; but he that was within answered that the animal was so heavy and unmanageable that he could not lift him from the ground, much less to the window. The other's impatience now increasing by the delay, he began to swear at his comrade for his clumsy awkwardness, and at last told him to give the business up if he could not do it quickly and come out of the stall; for if they stayed till daylight they would certainly be discovered. The other, with many oaths, replied that he believed it was the devil himself they had to deal with, for, said he, "I cannot now even get out myself, he has got such fast hold of me." The companion, daring to stay no longer, ran off, and left him to his fate. The fact was this: the Calf had been removed from the stall soon after the Thieves had seen it there, to make room for a Bear that had been brought into the town as a show; and it was this great beast that the Thief had the misfortune to encounter, and who kept hugging him till the morning, when he was discovered by the master of the Bear and taken to prison.

A knave may gain more than an honest man for a day, but the honest man will gain more than the knave for a year.

THE EAGLE AND THE OWL

The Eagle and the Owl, after many quarrels, swore that they would be friends forever, and that they would never harm each other's young ones. "But do you know my little ones?" said the Owl. "If you do not, I fear it will go hard with them when you find them." "No, I have never seen them," replied the Eagle. "The greater your loss," said the Owl; "they are the sweetest, prettiest things in the world. Such dear eyes! Such charming plumage! Such winning little ways! You'll know them, now, from my description." A short time after, the Eagle found the little Owls in a hollow tree. "These hideous, staring frights, at any rate, cannot be neighbor Owl's fine brood," said he; "so I may make away with them without the least misgiving." So saying he made a meal of them. The Owl, finding her young ones gone, loaded the Eagle with reproaches. "Nay," answered the Eagle, "blame yourself rather than me. If you paint with such flattering colors, it is not my fault if I do not recognize your portraits."

Love should not blind truth.

THE INDIAN AND THE FRENCHMAN

An airy Frenchman happened to meet an Indian upon the Mississippi, as he went, with his bow and arrow, to seek food for his family. Says Monsieur to the savage: "You have a very toilsome life of it; when other people sit by the fireside, enjoying good food and good company, you have to range the woods, in the midst of snow and storms, to preserve a wretched existence." "How come you by your food?" replied the Indian. "Does it rain from the clouds to you?" "No," says the

Frenchman; "we work in summer and make provision for the winter; and during the cold months sit by the fire and enjoy ourselves." "For the same reason," says the Indian, "we lay up food in winter that we may rest in summer, while the days are hot. What you account pleasure would be none to us; and your manner of life seems as ridiculous to the Indians as ours appears to you." The Frenchman could make no reply, and the Indian proceeded in his hunting. Custom has a mighty effect on mankind: and more differences in character arise from custom than from natural causes.

If all men are in the state they should be in, they should live contented.

THE OWL AND THE NIGHTINGALE

A formal solemn Owl had for many years made his habitation in a grove amongst the ruins of an old monastery, and had pored so often over some moldy manuscripts, the stupid relics of a monkish library, that he grew infected with the pride and pedantry of the place. Mistaking gravity for wisdom, he would sit whole days with his eyes half shut, fancying himself profoundly learned. It happened as he sat one evening, half buried in meditation and half in sleep, that a Nightingale, unluckily perching near him, began her melodious lays. He started from his reverie, and with a horrid screech interrupted her song. "Begone," cried he, "thou impertinent minstrel, nor distract with noisy dissonance my sublime contemplations; and know, vain songster, that harmony consists in truth alone, which is gained by laborious study; and not in languishing notes, fit only to soothe the ear of a lovesick maid." "Conceited pedant," returned the Nightingale, "whose wisdom lies only in the feathers that muffle up thy unmeaning face; music is a natural and rational entertainment, and though not adapted to the ears of an Owl, has ever been relished and admired by the best formed minds."

It is natural for a pedant to despise those arts that polish our manners, and that would extirpate pedantry.

THE MISER AND THE MAGPIE

As a Miser sat at his desk counting over his heaps of gold, a Magpie which had escaped from its cage picked up a coin and hopped away with it. The Miser, who never failed to count his money over the second time, immediately missed the piece, and rising up from his seat in the utmost consternation, observed the thief hiding it in a crevice in the floor. "And are you," cried he, "that worst of thieves, who has robbed me of my gold, without the plea of necessity and without regard to its proper use? Your life shall atone for so great a villainy!" "Soft words, good master," replied the Magpie; "have I, then, injured you in any other sense than you defraud the public? And am I not using your money in the same way that you do? If I must lose my life for hiding a single coin, pray what do you deserve, who secrets so many thousands?"

Remember your own infirmities when correcting those of others.

THE TWO FOXES

Two Foxes once found their way into a hen-roost, where they killed the Cock, the Hens, and the Chickens, and began to feed upon them. One of the Foxes, who was young and inconsiderate, was for devouring them all upon the spot; the other, who was old and covetous, proposed to reserve some of them for another time. "For experience, child," said he, "has made me wise, and I have seen many unexpected events since I came into the world. Let us provide therefore, against what may happen, and not consume all our stores at one meal." "All this is wondrous wise," replied the young Fox, "but for my part I am resolved not to stir until I have eaten as much as will serve me a whole week; for who would be mad enough to return hither, where it is certain the owner of these fowls will watch for us, and if he catch us, will put us to death?" After this short discourse, each pursued his own scheme. The young Fox ate till he burst himself, and had scarcely strength enough to reach his hole before

The Two Foxes

he died. The old one who thought it much better to deny his appetite for the present, and lay up provision for the future, returned the next day, and was killed by the farmer. Thus the young one came to grief through greed, and the old one through avarice.

Every age has its peculiar vice.

THE ROBIN AND THE SPARROW

As a Robin was singing on a tree by the side of a rural cottage, a Sparrow perched upon the thatch took occasion thus to reprimand him: "And dost thou," said he, "with thy dull autumnal note, presume to emulate the Birds of Spring? Can thy weak warblings pretend to vie with the sprightly accents of the Thrush and Blackbird, with the various melodies of the Lark or Nightingale, whom other birds far thy superiors, have long been content to admire in silence?" "Judge with candor at least," replied the Robin, "nor impute those efforts to ambition solely, which may sometimes flow from the love of art. I reverence, indeed, but by no means envy, the birds whose fame has stood the test of ages. Their songs have charmed both hill and dale, but their season is past, and their throats are silent. I feel not, however, the ambition to surpass or equal them; my efforts are of a much humbler nature, and I may surely hope for pardon, while I endeavor to cheer these forsaken valleys, by an attempt to imitate the strains I love."

Imitation may be pardonable where emulation would be presumptuous.

THE EAGLE, THE JACKDAW, AND THE MAGPIE

The kingly Eagle kept his court with all the formalities of state, which was duly attended by all his plumed subjects in their highest feathers. But these solemn assemblies were frequently disturbed by the impertinent conduct of two, who assumed the importance of highfliers, and these were no other than the Jackdaw and the Magpie, who were forever contending for precedence which neither of them would give up to the other. The contest ran so high that at length they mutually agreed to appeal to the sovereign Eagle for his decision in this momentous affair. The Eagle gravely announced that he did not wish to make any invidious distinction by deciding to the advantage of either party, but would give them a rule by which they might determine it between themselves. "In the future," said he, "the greater fool shall always take the lead; but which of you it may be, I leave you to settle."

Be not great in your own eyes, lest someone else deem you a fool.

INDUSTRY AND SLOTH

An indolent young man, being asked why he lay in bed so long, jocosely and carelessly answered: "Every morning of my life I hear long causes. I have two fine girls, their names are Industry and Sloth, close at my bedside, as soon as ever I awake, pressing their different suits. One entreats me to get up, the other persuades me to lie still; and then they alternately give me various reasons why I should rise, and why I should not. In the meantime, as it is the duty of an impartial judge to hear all that can be said on either side; before the pleadings are over, it is time to go to dinner."

The lazy have more excuses for their sloth than the productive have for their industry.

THE FOX AND THE CAT

A Fox and a Cat, traveling together, beguiled the tediousness of their journey by moralizing. "Of all the moral virtues," exclaimed the Fox, "mercy is surely the noblest! What say you, my sage friend, is it not so?"

"Undoubtedly," replied the Cat, with a most demure countenance; "nothing is more becoming in a creature of any sensibility than compassion." While they were thus complimenting each other on the wisdom of their views, a Wolf darted out from a wood upon a flock of Sheep which were feeding in an adjacent meadow, and without being in the least affected by the piteous cries of a poor Lamb, devoured it before their eyes. "Horrible cruelty!" exclaimed the Cat. "Why does he not feed on vermin, instead of making his barbarous meals on such innocent creatures?" The Fox agreed with his friend in the observation, to which he added some very pathetic remarks on the odiousness of such conduct. Their indignation was rising in its warmth and zeal when they arrived at a little cottage by the wayside, where the tender-hearted Fox immediately cast his eye upon a fine Cock that was strutting about in the yard. And now, adieu moralizing, he leaped over the pales, and without any sort of scruple, demolished his prize in an instant. In the meanwhile, a plump Mouse, which ran out of the stable, totally put to flight our Cat's philosophy, who fell to the repast without the least commiseration.

It is a common habit to talk of what is right and good, and to do what is quite the reverse.

THE GNAT AND THE BEE

A Gnat, half starved with cold and hunger, went one frosty morning to a beehive to beg charity; and offered to teach music in the Bee's family for her food and lodging. The Bee very civilly desired to be excused, "For," said she, "I bring up all my children to my own trade, that they may be able to get their living by their industry; and I am sure I am right, for see what that music, which you would teach my children, has brought you yourself to."

The worth of a calling is shown by its benefits.

THE DOGS AND THE HIDES

Some Dogs, famished with hunger, saw some cowhides steeping in a river. Not being able to reach them, they agreed to drink up the river: but it fell out that they burst themselves with drinking long before they reached the hides.

Attempt not impossibilities.

THE CAT AND THE BAT

A Cat, having devoured a favorite Bullfinch of her master's, over-heard him threatening to put her to death the moment he could find her. In this distress she offered a prayer to Jupiter, vowing, if he would deliver her from her present danger, that never while she lived would she eat another bird. Not long afterwards a Bat most invitingly flew into the room where puss was purring in the window. The question was, how to act upon so tempting an occasion? Her appetite pressed hard on one side, and her vow threw some scruples in her way on the other. At length she hit upon a most convenient distinction to remove all difficulties, by determining that as a bird indeed it was an unlawful prize, but as a mouse she might very con-scientiously eat it, and accordingly without further debate fell to the repast. Thus it is that men are apt to impose upon themselves by vain and groundless distinctions, when conscience and principle are at variance with interest and inclination.

Inclination gets the best of duty when we seek to
find it in books of casuistry.

THE PARTIAL JUDGE

A Farmer came to a neighboring Lawyer expressing great concern for an accident that, he said, had just happened. "One of your oxen," continued he, "has been gored by an unlucky bull of mine, and I should be glad to know how I am to make you reparation." "You are a very honest fellow," replied the Lawyer, "and will not think it unreasonable that I expect one of your oxen in return." "It is no more than justice," quoth the Farmer, "to be sure; but what did I say? I mistake—it is your bull that has killed one of my oxen." "Indeed," said the Lawyer, "that alters the case; I must inquire into the affair, and if——." "And if!" said the Farmer—"the business, I find, would have been concluded without an if, had you been as ready to do justice to others as to exact it from them."

Those who expect justice should be ready to accord it.

THE DOG AND THE CROCODILE

A Dog, running along the banks of the Nile, grew thirsty, but fearing to be seized by the monsters of that river, he would not stop to quench his thirst, but lapped as he ran. A Crocodile, raising his head above the surface of the water, asked him why he was in such a hurry? "I have often wished to meet you," added he, "and feel sure I should like you immensely. So why not stay and chat a while?" "You do me great honor," replied the Dog, "but I am afraid the pleasure would be all on your side; and, to tell the truth, it is to avoid such companions as you that I am in such haste."

We can never be too carefully guarded against a connection with persons of bad character.

THE DIAMOND AND THE GLOW-WORM

A Diamond happened to fall from the solitaire of a young lady as she was walking one evening on a terrace in her garden. A Glow-worm, who had beheld it sparkle in its descent soon as the gloom of night had eclipsed its luster, began to mock and to insult it. "Art thou that wondrous thing that vaunteth of such prodigious brightness? Where now is all thy boasted brilliancy? Alas, in an evil hour has fortune

The Dog and the Crocodile

thrown thee within the reach of my superior blaze." "Conceited insect," replied the gem, "that oweth thy feeble glimmer to the darkness that surrounds thee; know that my luster bears the test of day, and even derives its chief advantage from that distinguishing light, which discovers thee to be no more than a dark and paltry worm."

To be set in a strong point of light is as favorable
to merit as it is to imposture.

THE PEASANT AND THE APPLE TREE

A Peasant had in his garden an Apple tree, which bore no fruit, but only served as a harbor for the Sparrows and Grasshoppers. He resolved to cut it down and, taking his axe in his hand, made a bold stroke at its roots. The Grasshoppers and Sparrows entreated him not to cut down the tree that sheltered them, but to spare it, and they would sing to him and lighten his labors. He paid no attention to their request, but gave the Tree a second and a third blow with his axe; when he reached the hollow of the Tree, he found a hive full of honey. Greatly delighted, he threw down his axe, and thereafter took great care of the Tree.

Self-interest alone moves some men.

THE BLIND MAN AND THE WHELP

A Blind Man was accustomed to distinguish different animals by touching them with his hands. The whelp of a Wolf was brought him, with a request that he would feel it, and say what it was. He felt it, and being in doubt, said: "I do not quite know whether it is the cub of a Fox, or the whelp of a Wolf; but this I know full well that it would not be safe to admit him to the sheep fold."

Evil tendencies are shown in early life.

THE TOAD AND THE MAYFLY

As some workmen were digging marble in a mountain of Scythia, they discerned a Toad of an enormous size in the midst of a solid rock. They were very much surprised at so uncommon an appearance, and the more they considered the circumstances of it, the more their wonder increased. It was hard to conceive by what means this creature had preserved life and nourishment in so narrow a prison; and still more difficult to account for his birth and existence in a place so totally inaccessible to all of his species. They could conclude no other, than that he was formed together with the rock in which he had been bred, and was coeval with the mountain itself. While they were pursuing these speculations the Toad sat swelling and bloating, till he was ready to burst with pride and self-importance; to which at last he thus gave vent: "Yes," said he, "you behold in me a specimen of the antediluvian race of animals. I was begotten before the flood; and who is there among the present upstart race of mortals that shall dare to contend with me in nobility of birth or dignity of character?" A Mayfly sprung that morning from the river Hypanis, as he was flying about from place to place, chanced to be present, and observed all that passed with great attention and curiosity. "Vain boaster," said he, "what foundation hast thou for pride, either in thy descent, merely because it is ancient; or thy life, because it hath been long? What good qualities hast thou received from thy ancestors? Insignificant even to thyself, as well as useless to others, thou art almost as insensible as the block in which thou wast bred. Even I, that had my birth only from the scum of the neighboring river, at the rising of this day's sun, and who shall die at its setting, have more reason to applaud my condition, than thou hast to be proud of thine. I have enjoyed the warmth of the sun, the light of the day, and the purity of the air; I have flown from stream to stream, from tree to tree, and from the plain to the mountain; I have provided for posterity, and shall leave behind me a numerous offspring to people the next age of tomorrow; in short, I have fulfilled all the ends of my being, and I have been happy. My whole life, it is true, is but of twelve hours; but even one hour of it is to be preferred to a thousand years of mere existence; or that have been spent, like thine, in sloth, ignorance, and stupidity."

A lazy reliance on the antiquity of a family is, by far, less honorable than an honest industry.

THE WOLF AND THE SHEPHERDS

A Wolf, chancing to pass a Shepherd's hut, saw some Shepherds making merry over a joint of mutton. "A pretty row," quoth he, "would these Men have raised if they had caught me at such a supper."

Men are apt to condemn in others the very thing they themselves practice.

THE FLY IN ST. PAUL'S CUPOLA

As a Fly was crawling leisurely up one of the columns of St. Paul's Cupola, she often stopped, surveyed, examined, and at last broke forth into the following exclamation. "Strange! That anyone who pretended to be an artist should ever leave so superb a structure with so many roughnesses unpolished!" "Ah, my friend!" said a very learned architect, who hung in his web under one of the capitals, "you should never decide of things beyond the extent of your capacity. This lofty building was not erected for such diminutive animals as you or me; but for creatures who are at least ten thousand times as large; to their eyes, it is very possible, these columns may seem as smooth, as to you appear the wings of your favorite Mistress."

We should never estimate things beyond our reach by the narrow standard of our own capacities.

THE SPECTACLES[11]

Jupiter one day, enjoying himself over a bowl of nectar and in a merry humor, determined to make mankind a present. Momus,[12] who was

The Wolf and the Shepherds

appointed to convey it to them, mounted on a rapid car, and was presently on earth. "Come hither," says he, "ye happy mortals, great Jupiter has opened for your benefit his all-gracious hands. It is true, he made you somewhat short-sighted, but to remedy that inconvenience, behold how he has favored you!" So saying, he unloosed his portmanteau; an infinite number of spectacles tumbled out, and mankind picked them up with great eagerness. There was enough for all; every man had his pair. But it was soon found that these spectacles did not represent objects to all mankind alike, for one pair was purple, another blue; one was white, and another black; some of the glasses were red, some green, and some yellow. In short, there were of all manner of colors, and every shade of color. However, notwithstanding this diversity, every man was charmed with his own, as believing it the best, and enjoyed in his opinion all the satisfaction of truth.

Our opinions of things are altogether as various as though each saw them through a different medium; our attachments to these opinions as fixed and firm are as though all saw them through the medium of truth.

THE TRAVELER

A Man traveling on foot chanced to see lying in the road before him several Adders who were basking in the sun. He started back, having nearly trod on them and, with much respect and compassion, walked out of the path to avoid hurting them. Continuing his journey, it was not long before he came to some Earthworms who had issued out of the ground after a shower and, unluckily for themselves, were in the midst of the road; for the Traveler, paying no attention to them, carelessly crushed them to death under his feet.

How little men are inclined to pay their respects to those who inspire neither hope nor fear.

THE WIDOW AND HER SHEEP

A certain poor Widow had one solitary Sheep. At shearing time, wishing to take his fleece, and to avoid expense, she sheared him herself, but used the shears so unskillfully that with the fleece she sheared the flesh. The Sheep, writhing with pain, said: "Why do you hurt me so, Mistress? What weight can my blood add to the wool? If you want my flesh, there is the butcher, who will kill me in a trice; but if you want my fleece and wool, there is the shearer, who will shear and not hurt me."

The least outlay is not always the greatest gain.

THE FIGHTING COCKS AND THE TURKEY

Two Cocks of the genuine game breed met by chance upon the confines of their respective walks. To such great and heroic souls the smallest matter imaginable affords occasion for dispute. They approached each other with pride and indignation; they looked defiant, they crowed a challenge, and immediately commenced a bloody battle. It was fought on both sides so fiercely, and they received such deep wounds, that both lay down upon the turf utterly spent, blinded, and disabled. While this was their situation, a Turkey that had been a spectator of all that passed between them, drew near to the field of battle and reproved them in this manner: "How foolish and absurd has been your quarrel, my good neighbors! A more ridiculous one could scarce have happened among the most contentious of all creatures, men. Because you have crowed, perhaps, in each other's hearing, or because one of you has picked up a grain of corn upon the territories of his rival, you have both rendered yourselves miserable for the remainder of your days."

There is nothing so foolish as an idle quarrel.

THE BOY AND THE NETTLE

A Boy was stung by a Nettle. He ran home and told his mother, saying, "Although it pains me so much, I did but touch it ever so gently." "That was just what caused it to sting you," replied his mother. "The next time you touch a Nettle, grasp it boldly, and it will be soft as silk to your hand, and not hurt you in the least."

Whatsoever you do, do with all your might.

THE MONSTER IN THE SUN

An Astronomer was observing the Sun through a telescope in order to take an exact draft of the several spots which appear upon the face of it. While he was intent upon his observations, he was on a sudden surprised with a new and astonishing appearance; a large portion of the surface of the Sun was at once covered by a monster of enormous size and horrible form; it had an immense pair of wings, a great number of legs, and a long and vast proboscis; and that it was alive was very apparent, from his quick and violent motions, which the observer could from time to time plainly perceive. Being sure of the fact (for how could he be mistaken in what he saw so clearly?) our Philosopher began to draw many surprising conclusions from premises so well established. He calculated the magnitude of this extraordinary animal, and found that he covered about two square degrees of the Sun's surface; that placed upon the earth he would spread over half one hemisphere of it; and that he was seven or eight times as big as the moon. But what was most astonishing was the prodigious heat that he must endure; it was plain that he was something of the nature of the salamander, but of a far more fiery temperament; for it was demonstrable from the clearest principles, that in his present situation he must have acquired a degree of heat two thousand times exceeding that of red hot iron. It was a problem worth considering, whether he subsisted upon the gross vapors of the Sun, and so from time to time cleared away those spots which they are perpetually forming, and which would otherwise wholly obscure and incrustate its face; or whether it might not feed on the solid substance of the orb itself, which by this means, together with the constant expense of light, must soon be exhausted and consumed; or whether he was not now and then supplied by the falling of some eccentric Comet into the Sun. However this might be, he found by computation that the earth would be but short allowance for him for a few months; and farther, it was no improbable conjecture, that, as the earth was destined to be destroyed by fire, this fiery flying Monster would remove hither at the appointed time, and might much more easily and conveniently effect a conflagration than any Comet hitherto provided for that service. In the earnest pursuit of these, and many the like deep and curious speculations, the Astronomer was engaged, and was preparing to communicate them to the public. In the meantime, the discovery began to be much talked of, and all the virtuosi gathered together to see so strange a sight. They were equally convinced of the accuracy of the observation, and of the conclusions so clearly deduced from it. At last, one, more cautious than the rest, was resolved, before he gave a full assent to the report of his senses, to examine the whole process of the affair, and all the parts of the instrument; he opened the Telescope, and behold! A small Fly was inclosed in it, which having settled on the center of the object-glass had given occasion to all this marvelous Theory.

We should never estimate things beyond our reach by the narrow standard of our own capacities.

THE VILLAGE QUACK

A waggish, idle fellow in a country town, being desirous of playing a trick on the simplicity of his neighbors, and at the same time to put a little money in his pocket at their cost, advertised that he would on a certain day show a wheel carriage that should be so contrived as to go without horses. By silly curiosity the rustics were taken in, and each succeeding group who came out from the show were ashamed to confess to their neighbors that they had seen nothing but a wheelbarrow.

What artful knavery one half of the world would impose upon the folly of the other.

THE BEAR AND THE FOWLS

A Bear, who was bred in the forest, had an inclination to see the world. He traveled from one kingdom to another, making many profound observations on his way. One day he chanced to go into a farmer's yard, where he saw a number of Fowls standing to drink by the side of a pool. Observing that after every sip they turned up their heads towards the sky, he could not forbear inquiring the reason of so peculiar a ceremony. They told him that it was by way of returning thanks to Heaven for the benefits they received; and was, indeed, an ancient and religious custom, which they could not, with a safe conscience, or without impiety, omit. Here the Bear burst into a fit of laughter, at once mimicking their gestures and ridiculing their superstition in the most contemptuous manner. On this the Cock, with a spirit suitable to the boldness of his character, addressed him in the following words: "As you are a stranger, sir, you may perhaps be excused the rudeness of your behavior; yet give me leave to tell you that none but a Bear would ridicule any religious ceremonies whatsoever in the presence of those who believe them of importance."

Do not ridicule the creeds of others.

THE SPIDER AND THE SILKWORM

A Spider busied in spreading his web from one side of the room to the other was asked by an industrious Silkworm to what end he spent so much time and labor, in making such a number of lines and circles?

The Spider angrily replied, "Do not disturb me, thou ignorant thing; I transmit my ingenuity to posterity, and fame is the object of my wishes." Just as he had spoken, Susan the chambermaid, coming into the room to feed her silkworms, saw the Spider at his work and, with one stroke of her broom, swept him away and destroyed at once his labors and his hopes of fame.

He that is employed in works of use generally advantages himself or others; while he who toils for fame alone must expect often to lose his labor.

THE CONCEITED OWL

A young Owl, having accidentally seen himself in a crystal fountain, conceived the highest opinion of his personal perfections. "It is time," said he, "that Hymen should give me children as beautiful as myself, to be the glory of the night, and the ornament of our groves. What pity would it be if the race of the most accomplished of birds should be extinct for my want of a mate! Happy the female who is destined to spend her life with me!" Full of these self-approving thoughts, he entreated the Crow to propose a match between him and the royal daughter of the Eagle. "Do you imagine," said the Crow, "that the noble Eagle, whose pride it is to gaze on the brightest of the heavenly luminaries, will consent to marry his daughter to you, who cannot so much as open your eyes whilst it is daylight?" But the conceited Owl was deaf to all that his friend could urge; who, after much persuasion, was at length prevailed upon to undertake the commission. His proposal was received in the manner that might be expected: the king of birds laughed him to scorn. However, being a monarch of some humor, he ordered him to acquaint the Owl that if he would meet him the next morning at sunrise in the middle of the sky, he would consent to give him his daughter in marriage. The presumptuous Owl undertook to perform that condition; but being dazzled with the sun, and his head growing giddy, he fell from his height upon a rock; from whence being pursued by a flight of birds,

The Conceited Owl

he was glad at last to make his escape into the hollow of an old oak, where he passed the remainder of his days in that obscurity for which nature designed him.

Schemes of ambition, without proper talent, always end in disgrace.

THE ANGLER AND THE SALMON

An Angler on the margin of a river was fishing for the smaller kind of fish, and therefore had furnished himself with such delicate tackle that his hook was fixed to one single hair. Now it chanced that he hooked a large Salmon which, he concluded, would have proved the destruction of his slender apparatus; however, by judicious management he so gently played with his prey in giving it way and avoiding any act of violence, that at last he fairly conquered this huge fish, and drew it safely to the shore, exhausted by its own ineffectual efforts to get free. Thus the large Salmon had not strength enough to resist the power of a single hair.

Much may be done by a patient and prudent conduct where
violence would fail.

THE THREE VASES

By a lifetime of scraping, a Miser once hoarded up a large quantity of gold, which he placed in three Vases and buried. When at length, being on his deathbed, he called his three sons to him, and informed them of the treasure he had left them, and of the spot in which it lay hid, in three separate Vases—one for each of them—he could not finish all he had to say; a fainting fit seized him, and he expired. Now, as the young men had never seen these Vases, they concluded that in all probability they would differ in size and value; and as their father died before he could assign to each his particular Vase, that business must be settled by themselves. Thus, on the division of their wealth they entered into warm dispute, each laying claim to the largest Vase—one because he was the eldest; the second son because he had no property in lands to support him; and the youngest because he was the favorite of his father, and therefore was sure the largest share would have been bequeathed to him, had his dying parent been but able to finish his last speech. Words at length ran very high, and quickly came to blows, from which none of them escaped unhurt; when, after all this wrangle, ill-blood, and mischief done, it was discovered, on digging up the three Vases, that they were exactly equal in size and value.

Be sure of your cause before you quarrel.

HONOR, PRUDENCE, AND PLEASURE

Honor, Prudence, and Pleasure undertook to keep house together. Honor was to govern the family, Prudence to provide for it, and Pleasure to conduct its arrangements. For some time they went on exceedingly well, and with great propriety; but after a while Pleasure, getting the upper hand, began to carry mirth to extravagance, and filled the house with gay, idle, riotous company, and the consequent expenses threatened the ruin of the establishment; so that Honor and Prudence, finding it absolutely necessary to break up the partnership, determined to quit the house and leave Pleasure to go on her own way, which did not continue long, as she soon brought herself to poverty, and came a-begging to her former companions, who had now settled in another habitation. However, Honor and Prudence would never afterward admit Pleasure to be a partner in their household, but sent for her occasionally on holidays to make them merry, and in return they maintained her out of their alms.

Intemperance has an alluring aspect but a dreadful retinue.

THE BEE AND THE CUCKOO

A Bee flying out of his hive said to a Cuckoo, who was chanting on a bush hard by, "Peace! Why do you not leave off your monotonous pipe? There never was a bird who had such a tiresome, unvaried song as you have, 'Cuckoo, cuckoo, cuckoo' and 'Cuckoo,' again and again." "Oh," cried the Cuckoo, "I wonder you find fault with my note, which is as much varied as your labors, for if you had a hundred hives to fill, you would make them all exactly alike; if I invent nothing new, surely everything you do is as old as the creation of the world." To which the Bee replied, "I admit it, for in useful arts the want of variety is never in objection. But in works of taste and amusement, monotony is of all things to be avoided."

Those who do not have the capacity to judge works of art and taste expose themselves to ridicule when they play the critic.

THE CATS AND THE MONKEY

Two Cats, having stolen some cheese, could not agree about dividing the prize. In order, therefore, to settle the dispute, they consented to refer the matter to a Monkey. The proposed judge very readily accepted the office and, producing a balance, put a part into each scale. "Let me see," said he, "ah—this lump outweighs the other." And he bit off a considerable piece in order to make it balance. The opposite scale was now the heavier, which afforded our conscientious judge reason for a second mouthful. "Hold, hold!" said the two Cats, who began to be alarmed for the event, "give us our respective shares and we are satisfied." "If you are satisfied," returned the Monkey, "justice is not; a cause of this nature is by no means so soon determined." He continued to nibble first one piece then the other, till the poor Cats, seeing their cheese gradually diminishing, entreated him to give himself no further trouble, but to award them what remained. "Not so fast, I beseech you, friends," replied the Monkey; "we owe justice to ourselves as well as to you.

The Cats and the Monkey

What remains is due to me as a fee." Upon which he crammed the whole into his mouth, and with great gravity dismissed the court.

Those who dance must pay the piper.

THE SPANIEL AND THE MASTIFF

A good-natured Spaniel overtook a surly Mastiff as he was traveling upon the high road. The Spaniel, although a complete stranger to the Mastiff, very civilly accosted him; and if it would be no intrusion, he said, he should be glad to bear him company on his way. The Mastiff, who happened not to be altogether in so growling a mood as usual, accepted the proposal, and they very amicably pursued their journey together. In the midst of their conversation they arrived at the next village, where the Mastiff began to display his ugly temper by an unprovoked attack upon every Dog he met. The villagers immediately sallied forth with great indignation to rescue their pets; and falling upon our two friends without distinction or mercy, most cruelly treated the poor Spaniel for no other reason but his being found in bad company.

Much of every man's good or ill fortune depends upon his choice of friends.

THE SHEPHERD AND THE SHEEP

A Shepherd driving his Sheep to a wood saw an oak of unusual size, full of acorns, and spreading his cloak under the branches, he climbed up into the tree, and shook down the acorns. The Sheep eating them carelessly tore the cloak. The Shepherd coming down, and seeing what was done, said: "O you ungrateful creatures! You provide wool to make garments for all other men, but you destroy the clothes of him who feeds you."

Carelessness is a form of ingratitude.

THE COUNCIL OF HORSES

Once upon a time, a brash young Colt dissatisfied with the lot of his kind complained loudly to the Council of Horses: "How abject is our race! Are we condemned to slavery and servitude because our sires so willingly bore the chain? Is it right that Men should exploit our strength? Were we created only to serve their needs—dragging their plowshares, sweating in their harnesses, groaning beneath the loads they pile upon our backs? Reject the rein and spurn the spur! Let us be like the lion and the tiger and assert our claim to freedom and independence." Neighs of assent broke out among the assembled horses, and there was a great pawing of the ground in applause. But all were silenced when a Steed of great age and long experience addressed the assembly thus: "When I had the health and strength of my youth, I toiled as you do. Now, my grateful owner rewards my past pains by allowing me to roam freely and to feed on the crops yielded by the fields I once plowed. It is true that Man expects us to lend our pains to his endeavors, but does he not divide his care through all our labors of the year? Does he not provide us with buildings to shield us from the inclement weather and to keep our hay dry? Does he not share with us the bounty of the harvest? Since it is decreed that all creatures should help one another, ought we not be happy with our lot?" Seeing the wisdom of what their elder said, the Horses previously fired by the young Colt's discontent agreed, and the tumult ceased.

Those who know their station in life know the greatest contentment.

THE FARMER AND HIS DOG

A Farmer who had gone into his field to mend a gap in one of his fences found, at his return, the cradle in which he had left his only child asleep turned upside down, the clothes all torn and bloody, and his Dog lying near it, besmeared also with blood. Thinking that the animal had destroyed his child, he instantly dashed out his brains with the hatchet in his hand. When turning up the cradle, he found his

The Farmer and his Dog

child unhurt, and an enormous Serpent lying dead on the floor, killed by that faithful Dog, he lamented that the beast's courage and fidelity in preserving the life of his son deserved another kind of reward.

It is dangerous to give way to the blind impulse of a sudden passion.

THE MONKEY AND THE CAMEL

The Beasts of the forest gave a splendid entertainment at which the Monkey stood up and danced. Having vastly delighted the assembly, he sat down amid universal applause. The Camel, envious of the praises bestowed on the Monkey, and desirous to divert to himself the favor of the guests, proposed to stand up in his turn, and dance for their amusement. He moved about in so utterly ridiculous a manner, that the Beasts, in a fit of indignation, set upon him with clubs and drove him out of the assembly.

It is absurd to ape our betters.

THE WOODCOCK AND THE MALLARD

A Woodcock and a Mallard were feeding together in some marshy ground at the tail of a mill-pond. "Lord," said the squeamish Woodcock, "in what a voracious and beastly manner do you devour all that comes before you! Neither snail, frog, toad, nor any kind of filth, can escape the fury of your enormous appetite. All alike goes down, without measure and without distinction. What an odious vice is Gluttony!" "Good-lack!" replied the Mallard, "pray how came you to be my accuser? And whence has your excessive delicacy a right to censure my plain eating? Is it a crime to fill one's belly? Or is it not indeed a virtue rather, to be pleased with the food which nature offers us? Surely I would sooner be charged with gluttony, than with that finical and sickly appetite, on which you are pleased to ground your superiority of taste. What a silly vice is Daintiness!" Thus endeavoring to palliate their respective passions, our epicures parted with a mutual contempt. The Mallard hasting to devour some garbage, which was in reality a bait, immediately gorged a hook through mere greediness and oversight; while the Woodcock, flying through a glade, in order to seek his favorite juices, was entangled in a net, spread across it for that purpose; falling each of them thus a sacrifice to their different, but equal, foibles.

A voracious appetite, and a fondness for dainties, equally distract our attention for more material concerns.

THE FISHERMAN PIPING[13]

A Fisherman skilled in music took his flute and his nets to the seashore. Standing on a projecting rock he played several tunes, in the hope that the Fish, attracted by his melody would, of their own accord, dance into his net, which he had placed below. At last, having long waited in vain, he laid aside his flute, and casting his net into the sea, made an excellent haul of Fish. When he saw them leaping about in the net upon the rock he said: "O, you most perverse creatures, when I piped you would not dance, but now that I have ceased you do so merrily."

He achieves most who sticks to his trade.

MERCURY AND THE TRAVELER

A Man, about to depart upon a long journey, prayed to the god Mercury, who was anciently supposed to speed Travelers, to give him good voyage and a safe return. He promised Mercury that, if he would grant his request, he would give the god half of everything he might find on his road. Soon after he set forth, he found a bag of dates and almonds, which some passerby had lost. He ate all but the stones of the dates and the shells of the almonds at once. These he laid upon a wayside altar to the god; praying him to take notice that he had kept his promise. "For," said he, "here are the insides of the one, and the outsides of the other, and that makes up your half of the booty."

A promise-breaker is never at a loss for an excuse.

THE HOUNDS IN COUPLES

A Huntsman was leading forth his Hounds one morning to the chase and had linked several of the young dogs in couples to prevent their following every scent and hunting disorderly, as their own inclinations and fancy should direct them. Among others, it was the fate of Jowler and Vixen to be thus yoked together. Jowler and Vixen were both young and inexperienced, but had for some time been constant companions, and seemed to have entertained a great fondness for each other; they used to be perpetually playing together, and in any quarrel that happened, always took one another's part; it might have been expected, therefore, that it would not be disagreeable to them to be still more closely united. However, in fact, it proved otherwise; they had not been long joined together before both parties began to express uneasiness at their present situation. Different inclinations and opposite wills began to discover and to exert themselves: if one chose to go this way, the other was as eager to take the contrary; if one was pressing forward, the other was sure to lag behind; Vixen pulled back Jowler, and Jowler dragged along Vixen; Jowler growled at Vixen, and Vixen snapped at Jowler, till at last it came to a downright quarrel between them; and Jowler treated Vixen in a very rough and ungenerous manner, without any regard to the inferiority of her strength, or the tenderness of her sex. As they were thus continually vexing and tormenting one another, an old hound, who had observed all that passed, came up to them, and thus reproved them: "What a couple of silly puppies you are, to be perpetually worrying yourselves at this rate! What hinders your going on peaceably and quietly together? Cannot you compromise the matter between you by each consulting the other's inclination a little? At least, try to make a virtue of necessity, and submit to what you cannot remedy; you cannot get rid of the chain, but you may make it fit easy upon you. I am an old dog, and let my age and experience instruct you; when I was in the same circumstances with you, I soon found that thwarting my companion was only tormenting myself; and my yokefellow happily came into the same way of thinking. We endeavored to join in the same pursuits, and to follow one another's inclinations, and so we jogged on together, not only with ease and quiet, but with comfort and pleasure. We found by experience that mutual compliance not only compensates for liberty, but is even attended with a satisfaction and delight, beyond what liberty itself can give."

Mutual compliances are necessary to matrimonial happiness.

AESOP AND THE POULTRY

The populace of the neighborhood in which Aesop was a slave one day observed him attentively overlooking some poultry in an enclosure that was near the roadside; and those speculative wits who spend more time in prying into other people's concerns to no purpose than in adjusting their own were moved with curiosity to know why this philosopher should bestow his attention on those animals. "I am struck," replied Aesop, "to see how mankind so readily imitates this foolish animal." "In what?" asked the neighbors. "Why, in crowing well and scraping so ill," rejoined Aesop.

It is easier by far to talk boldly and make a noisy boast of one's merits than it is to act nobly or demonstrate worth by palpable acts.

THE SPORTSMAN AND THE SPANIEL

As a Sportsman ranged the field with his gun, attended by an experienced old spaniel, he happened to spring a Snipe and, almost at the same instant, a covey of Partridges. Surprised at the accident, and divided in his aim, he fired too indiscriminately, and by this

Aesop and the Poultry

means missed them both. "Oh, my good master," said the Spaniel, "you should never have two aims at once. Had you not been dazzled and seduced by the extravagant hope of bringing down a Partridge, you would probably have secured your Snipe."

We often miss our point by dividing our attention.

THE PEACOCK

The Peacock, who at first was distinguished only by a crest of feathers, preferred a petition to Juno that he might be honored also with a train. As the bird was a particular favorite, Juno readily enough assented; and his train was ordered to surpass that of every fowl in the creation. The Peacock, conscious of his superb appearance, thought it requisite to assume a proportionable dignity of gait and manners. The common poultry of the farmyard were quite astonished at his magnificence; and even the pheasants themselves beheld him with an eye of envy. But when he attempted to fly, he perceived himself to have sacrificed all his activity to ostentation; and that he was encumbered by the pomp in which he placed his glory.

The parade and ceremony belonging to the great are often a restraint upon their freedom and dignity.

THE WOLF AND THE HORSE

A Wolf coming out of a field of oats met a Horse and thus addressed him: "I would advise you to go into that field. It is full of capital oats, which I have left untouched for you, as you are a friend the very sound of whose teeth it will be a pleasure to hear." The Horse replied, "If oats had been the food of wolves, you would never have indulged your ears at the cost of your belly."

The deceitful reveal their true motives in the illogic of their schemes.

THE FATHER AND HIS TWO DAUGHTERS

A Man had two Daughters, one of whom married a Farmer, the other a Potter. After a while he paid a visit to the Farmer, and asked his Daughter how she was and if all was going well with her. "Splendidly," she replied, "I could wish for nothing more if only we had a little more rain for the crops." The same day, he went to the Potter's, and asked his other Daughter how things were faring at her new home. "Never better," she replied, "if only we had a little more fair weather to bake our clay." "Alack!" said the Father, "if you want shine and your sister rain, which am I to pray for on my own account?"

If all prayers were answered, no one would be satisfied.

THE EMIGRANT MICE

A Mouse, weary of living in the continual alarm attendant on the carnage committed among her nation by cats and traps, thus addressed herself to the tenant of a hole near her own: "An excellent thought has just come into my head; I read in some book which I gnawed a few days ago, that there is a fine country called the Indies, in which mice are in much greater security than here. In that region the sages believe that the soul of a mouse has been that of a king, a great captain, or some wonderful saint, and that after death it will probably enter the body of a beautiful woman or mighty potentate. If I recollect rightly, this is called metempsychosis. Under this idea they treat all animals with paternal charity, and build and endow hospitals for mice, where they are fed like people of consequence. Come then, my good sister, let us hasten to a country the customs of which are so excellent, and where justice is done to our merits." "But, sister," replied her neighbor, "do not cats enter these hospitals? If they do, metempsychosis must take place very soon, and in great numbers; and a talon or a tooth might make a fakir or a king, a miracle we can do very well without." "Do not fear," said the first mouse. "In these countries order is completely established; the cats have their houses as well as we ours, and they have their hospitals for the sick separate from ours." After

this conversation our two mice set out together, contriving the evening before they set sail to creep along the cordage of a vessel that was
to make a long voyage. They got under weigh, and were enraptured
with the sight of the sea that took them from the abominable shores
on which cats exercise their tyranny. The voyage was pleasant, and
they reached Surat, not like merchants to acquire riches, but to
receive good treatment from the Hindoos. They had scarcely entered
one of the houses fitted up for mice when they aspired to the best
accommodation. One of them pretended to recollect having formerly
been a Brahmin on the coast of Malabar, and the other protested that
she had been a fine lady of the same country, with long ears; but they
displayed so much impertinence that the Indian mice lost all patience.
A civil war commenced, and no quarter was given to the two new-
comers who pretended to impose laws on the others; when, instead of
being eaten up by cats, they were strangled by their own brethren.

It is useless to go far in search of safety if we are not modest and wise.

THE CUCKOO, THE HEDGE-SPARROW, AND THE OWL

A lazy Cuckoo, too idle to make a comfortable home for herself and
her offspring, laid her eggs in the nest built by the Hedge-Sparrow
who, taking the charge wholly on herself, hatched them, and bred up
the young with maternal attention, till such time as they were enabled
to provide for themselves, when they took wing and fled. Upon this
the worthless Cuckoo came gossiping to the Owl, complaining of the
misconduct of the Hedge-Sparrow in treating her with so little attention, in return for the confidence she had shown in entrusting her
with the care of her precious young brood. "Would you believe it?"
continued the Cuckoo. "The ungrateful birds have flown off without
paying me any of those duties which are the natural right of a mother
from her offspring!" "Peace, peace," replied the sage Owl, "nor expect
that from others which you cannot give in return. The obligation lies
wholly on your side to the charitable Hedge-Sparrow, for her kindness
to your helpless young, whom you had abandoned; and remember

this, that before you teach gratitude to others, you should learn yourself to be grateful."

Ne'er-do-wells always find flaws in their neighbors.

THE BLIND MAN AND THE LAME MAN

A Blind Man, being stopped in a bad piece of road, met with a Lame Man, and entreated him to guide him through the difficulty he had got into. "How can I do that?" replied the Lame Man, "since I am scarce able to drag myself along? But as you appear to be very strong, if you will carry me, we will seek our fortunes together. It will then be my interest to warn you of anything that may obstruct your way; your feet shall be my feet, and my eyes your eyes." "With all my heart," returned the Blind Man; "let us render each other our mutual services." So taking his lame companion on his back, they, by means of their union, traveled on with safety and pleasure.

From our wants and infirmities almost all the connections
of society take their rise.

THE BEES AND THEIR KEEPER

A Thief came into a Bee garden one day while the Keeper was away and robbed the hives. Not long afterward the Keeper returned and was greatly disturbed about the theft, not only because of the loss of honey, but also because the hives had been overturned. While he was busily at work trying to set the garden at rights, the Bees came home laden from the fields and, missing their combs, flew in angry swarms about their Master. "Foolish and ungrateful creatures!" exclaimed he. "You let a stranger who has robbed you escape unharmed, while you are ready to attack your best friend."

People too often mistake their friends for their foes.

The Blind Man and the Lame Man

THE BOWMAN AND THE LION

A Man who was very skillful with his bow went up into the mountains to hunt. At his approach there was instantly a great consternation and rout among all the wild beasts, the Lion alone showing any determination to fight. "Stop," said the Bowman to him, "and await my messenger, who has something to say to you." With that, he sent an arrow after the Lion, and wounded him in the side. The Lion, smarting with anguish, fled into the depth of the thickets, but a Fox seeing him run, bade him take courage, and face his enemy. "No," said the Lion, "you will not persuade me to that; for if the messenger he sends is so sharp, what must be the power of him who sends it?"

*The timid will always urge on to danger those more valiant
than themselves.*

THE SHEEP AND THE BRAMBLE

A Sheep, during a severe storm, wandered into a thicket for shelter, and there lay so snug and warm that he soon fell fast asleep. The clouds clearing away and the winds returning to rest inclined the Sheep to return to his pasture. But, ah! What was his situation: a Bramble had laid such a firm hold of his fleece that it was left as a forfeit for the protection the thicket had given him.

He who makes his bed must lie in it.

THE SWALLOW AND THE SERPENT

A Swallow, returning from abroad and ever fond of dwelling with men, built herself a nest in the wall of a Court of Justice, and there hatched seven young birds. A Serpent gliding past the nest from its hole in the wall ate up the young unfledged nestlings. The Swallow, finding her nest empty, lamented greatly, and exclaimed: "Woe to me a stranger! That in this place where all others' rights are protected, I alone should suffer wrong."

Do not place too great confidence in outward form.

THE LAMB IN THE TEMPLE

A Wolf pursued a Lamb, which fled for refuge to a certain Temple. The Wolf called out to him and said: "The Priest will slay you in sacrifice, if he should catch you," on which the Lamb replied: "It would be better for me to be sacrificed in the Temple, than to be eaten by you."

'Tis better to die for a good cause than for an evil one.

THE CAT AND THE BIRDS

A Cat, hearing that the Birds in a certain cage were ailing, dressed himself up as a physician and, taking with him his cane and the instruments becoming his profession, went to the cage, knocked at the door, and inquired of the inmates how they all did, saying that if they were ill, he would be happy to prescribe for them and cure them. They replied, "We are all very well, and shall continue so, if you will only be good enough to go away and leave us as we are."

Some cures are worse than the disease.

THE HUNTER, THE FOX, AND THE TIGER

A certain Hunter saw, in the middle of a field, a Fox whose skin was so beautiful that he wished to take him alive. Having this in view, he found out his hole, and just before the entrance to it he dug a large and deep pit, covered it with slender twigs and straw, and placed a

The Hunter, the Fox, and the Tiger

piece of horseflesh on the middle of the covering. When he had done this he went and hid himself in a corner out of sight, and the Fox, returning to his hole and smelling the flesh, ran up to see what dainty morsel it was. When he came to the pit he would fain have tasted the meat, but fearing some trick he refrained from doing so, and retreated into his hole. Presently up came a hungry Tiger, who, being tempted by the smell and appearance of the horseflesh, sprang in haste to seize it, and tumbled into the pit. The Hunter, hearing the noise made by the Tiger in falling, ran up and jumped into the pit without looking into it, never doubting that it was the Fox that had fallen in. But there, to his surprise, he found the Tiger, which quickly tore him in pieces and devoured him.

Look before you leap.

THE FLEA AND THE WRESTLER

A Flea settled upon the bare foot of a Wrestler, and bit him; on which the Wrestler called loudly upon Hercules for help. The Flea a second time hopped upon his foot, when the Wrestler groaned and said, "O Hercules! If you will not help me against a Flea, how can I hope for your assistance against greater antagonists?"

Help yourself in the little things, and Fortune will
help you in the greater.

THE HERMIT AND THE BEAR

A certain Hermit having done a good office to a Bear, the grateful creature was so sensible of his obligation, that he begged to be admitted as the guardian and companion of his solitude. The Hermit willingly accepted his offer; and conducting him to his cell they passed their time together in an amicable manner. One very hot day, the Hermit having laid him down to sleep, the officious Bear employed

The Hermit and the Bear

himself in driving away the flies from his friend's face. But in spite of all his care, one of the flies perpetually returned to the attack, and at last settled upon the hermit's nose. "Now I shall have you, most certainly," said the Bear; and with the best intentions imaginable, gave him a violent blow on the face, which very effectually indeed demolished the fly, but at the same time mangled in a most shocking manner his benefactor's face.

The random zeal of inconsiderate friends is often as hurtful as the wrath of enemies.

THE HORSE AND THE STAG[14]

The Horse having quarrelled with the Stag, and being unable to revenge himself upon his enemy, came to a Man and begged his help. He allowed the Man to saddle and bridle him, and together they ran down the Stag and killed him. The Horse neighed with joy, and, thanking his rider warmly, asked him now to remove his saddle and let him go. "No, no," said the Man; "you are much too useful to me as you are." The Horse thenceforward served the Man, and found that he had gratified his revenge at the cost of his liberty.

Put bounds to your anger or it will put bounds to you.

MINERVA'S OLIVE

The gods, say the heathen mythologists, have each of them their favorite tree. Jupiter preferred the oak, Venus the myrtle, and Phoebus the laurel; Cybele the pine, and Hercules the poplar. Minerva, surprised that they should choose barren trees, asked Jupiter the reason. "It is," said he, "to prevent any suspicion that we confer the honor we do them for the sake of their fruit." "Let folly suspect what it pleases," returned Minerva; "I shall not scruple to acknowledge, that I make choice of the olive for the usefulness of its fruit." "O daughter," replied the father of the gods, "it is with justice that men esteem thee wise; for nothing is truly valuable that is not useful."

Whatever fancy may determine, the standing value of all things is in proportion to their use.

THE OWL AND THE GRASSHOPPER

An Owl who was sitting in a hollow tree, dozing away a long summer's afternoon, was very much disturbed by a rogue of a Grasshopper who kept singing in the grass beneath. So far indeed from keeping quiet, or moving away at the request of the Owl, the Grasshopper sang all the more, and called her an old blinker that only came out at nights when all honest people were gone to bed. The Owl waited in silence for a short time, and then artfully addressed the Grasshopper as follows: "Well, my dear, if one cannot be allowed to sleep, it is something to be kept awake by such a pleasant little pipe as yours, which makes most agreeable music, I must say. And now I think of it, my mistress Pallas gave me the other day a bottle of delicious nectar. If you will take the trouble to come up, you shall have a drop, and it will clear your voice nicely." The silly Grasshopper, beside himself with the flattery, came hopping up to the Owl. When he came within reach, the Owl caught him, killed him, and finished her nap in comfort.

Flattery works better than threats.

The Owl and the Grasshopper

ENDNOTES

INTRODUCTION

1. (p. xv) http://www.creighton.edu/aesop/ for the Carlson Fable Collection which "includes over 6000 books and 4000 fable related objects" to get some idea of just how widespread the fables are.
2. (p. xvi) There are actually two versions of the *Life* that have come down from antiquity; they are similar but not identical. The most complete version can be found in Daly's *Aesop Without Morals*.
3. (p. xvii) The most detailed discussion of what the *Life* is and how it relates to other Greek writings is Leslie Kurke's book *Aesopic Conversations*.

THE FABLES

1. (p. 9) *THE BODY AND ITS MEMBERS:* This fable can be found in Roman historian Livy's *History of Rome*, in which it was used to reconcile the rulers and the people to each other by convincing the people that their rulers played an important role in the health of the body politic and did not merely consume what others produced. A longer and more detailed use of the imagery from this fable can also be found in 1 Corinthians 12: 12–31.
2. (p. 13) *THE COLLIER AND THE FULLER:* A collier's occupation was making charcoal, a notoriously smoky and dirty job, while a fuller's work involved cleaning woolen cloth. Thus, it would have been common sense for fullers to stay away from colliers.
3. (p. 24) *Tiberius Cæsar:* Tiberius Caesar was the second emperor of Rome, holding that position from 14 to 37 CE. Although a successful general, he was not a successful ruler. When he died, he was succeeded by the notorious Caligula (who may have been involved in Tiberius' death).
4. (p. 77) *MERCURY AND THE CARVER:* Jupiter was the king of the gods in Roman mythology, and Juno was his wife. Mercury was a god of trade and success in commerce, so his reference to being "a special patron of your craft" is as a seller of goods, not as a maker of goods.

5. (p. 112) *THE SATYR AND THE TRAVELER:* Satyrs were like human beings, but they also had some animal characteristics. Great lovers of wine, dancing, and sex, they were associated with Bacchus, who was the god of wine and the theater.

6. (p. 114) *THE FOX AND THE HEDGEHOG:* This fable is found in Aristotle's *Rhetoric* (mid-fourth century), in which Aristotle attributes it to Aesop. In *Rhetoric,* Aristotle puts the tale in a political context: Aesop is speaking to an assembly of the people and defending a demagogue accused of corruption. He is using this fable to argue that since this man is already rich, they have nothing more to fear from him, but if he is removed, he will be replaced by people eager for gain who will rob them further. Aristotle recommends the use of fables to persuade assemblies; it is often easier to construct a fable than it is to find a relevant historical example that will also be persuasive. (See also "The Horse and the Stag.")

7. (p. 115) *THE WOLF AND THE MASTIFF* and (p. 117) *THE NIGHTINGALE AND HIS CAGE:* Note that these two fables appear to have morals that are completely opposed to each other. The fable form allows for many messages to be communicated, and considering both of these fables at once should encourage the reader to reflect on the costs and benefits of freedom and the question of who is and is not suited for it.

8. (p. 122) *Pallas:* Pallas is another name for Athena, the Greek goddess of wisdom.

9. (p. 158) *THE ASTRONOMER:* This story can be found in Plato's dialogue *Theaetetus* (mid-fourth century), where Socrates claims that it happened specifically to the philosopher Thales, who was also an astronomer and was said to have accurately predicted an eclipse in 585 BCE. Socrates suggests that all philosophers are like this, although he may not have been serious about that.

10. (p. 180) *THE THRUSH AND THE FOWLER:* Birdlime is a sticky substance used to trap birds. The usual method is to spread it on twigs or reeds and wait for birds to land on it and become stuck. Here, the fowler is taking a more active role, using birdlime-covered reeds held in his hand to capture the bird that has foolishly left itself vulnerable.

11. (p. 197) *THE SPECTACLES:* This fable, like many others, explains how something in the world came to be a particular way: In this case we have a fable about why people have different opinions. But there is another element to the story. It suggests, without explicitly saying so, that although everyone sees the world differently, each individual believes that his or her own opinions are right and superior to those of others, ironically providing one opinion that everyone does share. Fables may be short, but they can have many layers of meaning.

12. (p. 197) *Momus:* Momus was the Roman god of blame, satire, and mockery.

13. (p. 214) *THE FISHERMAN PIPING:* This fable is found in Herodotus' *Histories.* Cyrus asks the people of Ionia to rebel against his enemy

Croesus. They refuse, but after Cyrus gains another victory against Croesus, they offer to be his subjects if he will give them the same conditions they currently have as subjects of Croesus. He replies with this fable, letting them know that they should have danced when he first asked them to and now they will be dancing to much less pleasant music.

14. (p. 228) *THE HORSE AND THE STAG:* This fable also appears in Aristotle's *Rhetoric* (along with "The Fox and the Hedgehog"), where it, too is given a political context: Having appointed Phalaris military dictator, the people of Himera have already let themselves be bridled; if they give him a group of soldiers for protection, they will become completely enslaved.

BASED ON THE BOOK

OTHER WRITINGS IN THE SAME GENRE

IF AESOP'S FABLES LEAVE YOU EAGER TO READ MORE ANIMAL STORIES from long ago, turn to India. Hailing from that land, the tales of both the Hindu *Panchatantra* and the Buddhist *Jātaka* date back thousands of years and use animal stories to educate and entertain. The two texts have some stories in common, suggesting that they may have had a common source. And, interestingly, they both contain tales that resemble Aesopic fables, as well. Scholars disagree about the degree to which the Greeks and Indians borrowed from one another; given that much fable transmission would have been oral and many of the earliest written texts we know of have since been lost, this is a disagreement that probably cannot be definitively settled. But we do know that in more recent times Western authors have borrowed from both the *Panchatantra* and the *Jātaka*, turning stories from these texts into fables of the kind found in this book.

Of the two texts, the *Panchatantra* is by far the more elaborate, in that it uses a frame story to organize a diverse array of tales—a literary device that will be familiar to anyone who has enjoyed the *Decameron* by Giovanni Boccaccio or Geoffrey Chaucer's *The Canterbury Tales*. The main story begins when a king with three sons, frustrated that they all remain exceedingly ignorant despite long attempts to impart them with knowledge, asks his counselors what can be done to educate them quickly. One counselor recommends that the king summon the wise Visnu Sarma and ask him to provide the necessary instruction. The King follows this advice, and Visnu Sarma successfully uses a series of eighty-seven animal stories, told over a period of six months, to teach the three princes about the duties and problems of kingship while giving them a practical education in how to rule and how to live. Many of Visnu Sarma's lessons are valuable even for people who are not rulers, and the *Panchatantra* has been extremely popular throughout India for millennia. It has also been disseminated around the world in a multitude of languages, often being adapted in the process so that the lessons it teaches are more culturally appropriate for the society receiving it. It was a source for the important Arabic collection of animal stories *Kalīlah wa Dimnah* and also for the well-known and beloved *Thousand and One Nights*. Some of the stories from the *Panchatantra* were adapted by the French author Jean de La Fontaine into a collection of fables in the late 1600s and have subsequently found their way into many fable collections in the English language.

The *Panchatantra* shares several similarities with Aesop's fables. The former's authorship is sometimes attributed to Visnu Sarma, but like Aesop, Visnu Sarma may never have existed. Like Aesop's fables, the *Panchatantra* may well have been the result of collective authorship, with different parts having been created and set down in writing by different people. This is plausible because, in another parallel with Aesop's fables, the *Panchatantra* was part of an oral tradition for some time before it was written down; the earliest known written text dates to the third century BCE, but scholars believe that the stories found in it are actually much older. And, as mentioned earlier, there are stories in the *Panchatantra* that resemble particular fables of Aesop. "The Elephants and the Mice" is similar to Aesop's "The Lion and the Mouse," and the story "The Brahmin and the Cobra" warns against greed in a way that recalls Aesop's "The Goose that Laid the Golden Eggs."

The *Jātaka* tales—there are 547 of them—go back to the fourth century BCE. In their original form, at least some of them may have been folk tales, but in the form in which we have them, they provide explicit instruction in Buddhist principles. (In this they resemble the fables, which originally circulated without explicit morals stated at the end, but which later had such lessons attached to them to suit the moral teachings of particular editors.) Unlike the *Panchatantra*, this collection is not shaped by an overarching narrative. Instead, there is a single unifying conceit, repeated at the outset of each tale: The Buddha is presented with an ethical or practical problem, the Buddha announces that this is not the first time that such a situation has occurred, and then he recounts an edifying exemplar from one of his many incarnations on the path to enlightenment. In 123 of the 547 tales, the Buddha is incarnated as some kind of animal—and more than three dozen different animals are represented in these 123 tales, some more than once. The *Jātaka* tales are similar to Aesop's fables in their form and in their frequent reliance on animals as the main characters. Moreover, their brevity and relative simplicity make them easy to remember and use, as is the case with Aesop's fables. The lay Buddhist, especially one who was poor and illiterate, would have had no chance to study lengthy and complicated Buddhist texts, but they could remember and apply the practical and moral lessons taught by the stories of the *Jātaka*. And, as is the case with the *Panchatantra*, some *Jātaka* tales are very similar to certain ones from Aesop. For example, in volume 1 of Robert Chalmers' collection of the *Jātaka* tales, fable 43 is about a viper that betrays its human benefactor which is a story very much like Aesop's "The Countryman and the Snake," and fable 30 is about the seemingly easy life of an animal being fattened for the slaughter, which recalls Aesop's "The Wanton Calf."

Reading these texts along with Aesop's fables helps to make clear the variety of ways in which animal stories have been used around the world for millennia. Some are funny, some are disturbing, and almost all are thought provoking. In reading stories about other animals, we are ultimately reading about ourselves, and being encouraged to think about the kind of animals we are and the appropriate way for such an animal to behave.

WRITINGS IN OTHER GENRES

Most modern authors working with Aesop's Fables are writing books for children, but authors also continue to find ways to use the fables to give advice to adults. Several of them have brought the fables to the world of business, hoping to advise their audience as to how to become top dog in one's field or just get ahead in the rat race. Two recent authors, David Lignell and David Noonan, take different approaches to this type of project. Lignell, in his book *Aesop in a Monkey Suit: Fifty Fables of the Corporate Jungle*, keeps the basic action of the fables, but changes the characters and settings to fit the corporate world. His efforts to modernize the fables are not always successful, as he occasionally struggles to fit the fables into business settings where they really don't belong. Yet sometimes it works: for example, the manager who successfully gives his employees a lesson in teamwork by demonstrating that a bundle of project reports tied together is impossible to tear in half while each report separately is easily destroyed conveys the same message as the old man gives his sons in the original fable "The Old Man and His Sons." Lignell includes the title of the original fable and a clear moral with each of his adaptations, but he offers neither the text of the original fable nor any additional commentary to go along with the new fables he has created. As a result, any wisdom to be found in this book comes from the original fables, and attentive readers would gain just as much from the original fables as they would from the versions explicitly targeted at people in the business world.

Much more successful is the second approach, in which the fable is kept in its original form but the author provides additional material—such as stories, examples, and commentary—to elaborate on the meaning of the fable and the context in which it can be useful. Noonan's *Aesop & the CEO* takes this approach. Each of Noonan's chapters (there are forty-seven) begins with one of Aesop's fables, followed by the moral usually associated with that fable; there is then a relevant business case, followed by a business moral. For example, in the case of the fable "The Old Man and His Sons," Noonan begins with the tale as it has traditionally been told (although he retitles it "The Bundle of Sticks"), and then gives the usual moral "In union there is strength." He follows this with a description of the team approach used effectively by the San Diego Zoo, and then offers the conclusion "It's good business to promote teamwork." This is much more effective than simply rewriting the fable. Readers are given clear examples of how the wisdom of the fables can be applied to business problems, drawn from actual organizations and events, and hopefully can use the fables in similar situations that they encounter for themselves.

WORKS CREATED IN OTHER MEDIUMS

Aesop's fables have been the basis of an enormous number of musical recordings, plays, films, and cartoons. Their brevity and simple plots, as well as their (seemingly) clear-cut moral statements, make them well suited for translation into many different mediums (as well as many different languages). There are far too many to note here; a list can be found at Father Greg Carlson's website at http://www.creighton.edu/aesop/artifacts/audiovisual/index.php.

Perhaps the best-known film adaptation of one of Aesop's fables is Warner Brothers' transformation of "The Hare and the Tortoise" into three short animated cartoons featuring Bugs Bunny as the hare and Cecil Turtle as the Tortoise. In the first two of these ("Tortoise Beats Hare," released in 1941, and "Tortoise Wins by a Hare," released in 1943), Cecil defeats Bugs in a race, just as the tortoise defeats the hare in the original fable. In the third ("Rabbit Transit," released in 1947), Bugs actually wins the race, but after Cecil gets him to announce that he was going one hundred miles per hour in a thirty-miles-per-hour zone, the police take him away to jail.

Also well known are the adaptations (often very loose adaptations) of the fables for the "Aesop and Son" short cartoons that were part of *The Rocky and Bullwinkle Show*, which originally aired from 1959 to 1964. In these cartoons, "Aesop" uses fables to teach his son important life lessons, with the morals invariably delivered in the form of terrible puns.

FURTHER READING

ADRADOS, FRANCISCO RODRIGUEZ. *History of the Graeco-Latin Fable*. Vols. 1 and 3. Leiden, NL: Brill, 2003.

BLACKHAM, H. J. *The Fable as Literature*. London: Athlone Press, 1985.

CARNES, PACK. *Fable Scholarship: An Annotated Bibliography*. New York: Garland Publishing, Inc., 1985.

COMPTON, TODD. *Victim of the Muses*. Cambridge, MA: Center for Hellenic Studies, 2006.

COWELL, E. B., ED. *The Jātaka or Stories of the Buddha's Former Births*. London: Routledge & Kegan Paul, 1973.

DALY, LLOYD. *Aesop Without Morals*. New York: Thomas Yoseloff, 1961.

HÄGG, TOMAS. "A Professor and His Slave: Conventions and Values in the *Life of Aesop*." In *Conventional Values of the Hellenistic Greeks*, edited by Per Bilde, Troels Engberg-Pedersen, Lise Hannestad, and Jan Zahle, 177–203. Aarhus, DK: Aarhus University Press, 1997.

HOLZBERG, NIKLAS. *The Ancient Fable: An Introduction*. Translated by Christine Jackson-Holzberg. Bloomington: Indiana University Press, 2002.

JONES, JOHN GARRETT. *Tales and Teachings of the Buddha: The Jātaka Stories in relation to the Pāli Canon*. London: George Allen & Unwin, 1979.

KURKE, LESLIE. *Aesopic Conversations*. Princeton: Princeton University Press, 2011.

LIGNELL, DAVID. *Aesop in a Monkey Suit: Fifty Fables of the Corporate Jungle*. New York: iUniverse, 2006.

LISSARRAGUE, FRANÇOIS. "Aesop, Between Man and Beast: Ancient Portraits and Illustrations." In *Not The Classical Ideal*, edited by Beth Cohen, 132–149. Leiden, NL: Brill, 2000.

NAGY, GREGORY. *The Best of the Achaeans.* Baltimore: Johns Hopkins University Press, 1979.

NOONAN, DAVID C. *Aesop & the CEO: Powerful Business Insights from Aesop's Ancient Fables.* Nashville, TN: Thomas Nelson, 2005.

PAPADEMETRIOU, J. TH A. *Aesop as an Archetypal Hero.* Athens: Hellenistic Society for Humanistic Study, 1997.

PATTERSON, ANNABEL. *Fables of Power: Aesopian Writing and Political History.* Durham, NC: Duke University Press, 1991.

PERRY, B. E. *Aesopica,* Vol. 1. Urbana: University of Illinois Press, 1952.

———. *Babrius and Phaedrus.* Cambridge, MA: Harvard University Press, 1965.

———. *Studies in the Text History of the Life and Fables of Aesop.* Chico, CA: Scholars Press, 1981.

PERVO, RICHARD. "A Nihilist Fabula: Introducing the *Life of Aesop.*" In *Ancient Fiction and Early Christian Narrative,* edited by Ronald F. Hock, J. Bradley Chance, and Judith Perkins, 77–120. Atlanta: Scholars Press, 1998.

PLATO. *Phaedo.* Translated by C. J. Rowe. Cambridge: Cambridge University Press, 1993.

VAN DIJK, GERT-JAN. *Ainoi, Logoi, Mythoi: Fables in Archaic, Classical, and Hellenistic Greek Literature.* Leiden, NL: Brill, 1997.

VISNU SARMA. *The Panchatantra.* Translated and with an introduction by Chandra Rajan. New York: Penguin Books, 1993.

WINKLER, JOHN J. *Auctor and Actor.* Berkeley: University of California Press, 1985.

ZAFIROPOULOS, CHRISTOS A. *Ethics in Aesop's Fables: The Augustana Collection.* Leiden, NL: Brill, 2001.

INDEX